Praise for *Taking the 5 Leaps*

The opportunity to read *Taking the 5 Leaps* came at a very important time for me, as I was personally feeling God ask me to leap into a new assignment. I had so many questions for God, and Rachel's thoroughly biblical explanation, specifically of the difference between calling and assignment, helped me see my situation with such clarity. If you're in a season where God is asking you to do something different, or even uncomfortable, do yourself a favor and read this book.

BROOKE MCGLOTHLIN, founder of Million Praying Moms and author of *Praying Mom: Making Prayer the First and Best Response to Motherhood*

Taking the 5 Leaps is an empowering guide to stepping out in faith and pursuing God's calling. With vulnerability and wisdom, Rachel shares personal stories and biblical examples that will resonate with anyone seeking to follow God's lead into new territory. This book outlines a thoughtful process, equipping readers to prepare spiritually, emotionally, logistically, and financially for their leap. Rachel offers practical advice for discerning God's voice, overcoming fear, and persevering through challenges. Her insights on timing, community, and resting in God's provision are invaluable. Whether you feel called to ministry, a career change, or simply a new season, *Taking the 5 Leaps* will inspire courage and faith. We highly recommend this book and for everyone to accept Rachel's gentle push to move past comfort zones and step into God's plan.

SCOTT & VANESSA MARTINDALE, bestselling authors; founders of Blended Kingdom Families and SEVN Therapy Co.

What often appears to be a daring leap really only requires a step of faith. Living (or leaping!) by faith is not about eliminating uncertainties but about entrusting them to the One who has gone before you. *Taking the 5 Leaps* is a powerful invitation to walk hand in hand with God, making our faith steps confidently because His faithfulness never fails.

MICHELLE MYERS, cohost of the *She Works His Way* podcast; author of the Conversational Commentary series, *She Works His Way,* and *Famous in Heaven and at Home*

As someone who has taken many leaps, I didn't have anything more to learn about taking leaps. So I thought. After only a few chapters into this book, I realized how wrong I was! Rachel teaches us to embrace, navigate, and courageously leap into our God-given callings. While reading this book, I realized I've been fearfully delaying a leap of faith in this season of my life. *Taking the 5 Leaps* has given me the wisdom and courage to leap boldly, and it will do the same for you. I highly recommend this book!

JACKIE BLEDSOE, author of *7 Rings of Marriage,* speaker, and entrepreneur

Taking the 5 Leaps by my friend Rachel G. Scott is an invaluable guide for anyone ready to embrace their God-given calling. Through biblical insights and personal stories, Rachel equips readers to move from hesitation to action, outlining five types of leaps they can take. This book is an invitation to make leaping a lifestyle, offering courage and wisdom for those seeking purpose and fulfillment in their work for the glory of God and the good of others.

JORDAN RAYNOR, bestselling author of *The Sacredness of Secular Work* and *Redeeming Your Time*

EXPERIENCING GOD'S FAITHFULNESS
AS YOU RESPOND TO HIS CALL

Taking the 5 Leaps

RACHEL G. SCOTT

MOODY PUBLISHERS
CHICAGO

Scripture quotations are from the ESV® Bible (The Holy Bible, English Standard Version®), © 2001 by Crossway, a publishing ministry of Good News Publishers. Used by permission. All rights reserved. The ESV text may not be quoted in any publication made available to the public by a Creative Commons license. The ESV may not be translated in whole or in part into any other language.

Scripture quotations marked (NLT) are taken from the Holy Bible, New Living Translation, copyright ©1996, 2004, 2015 by Tyndale House Foundation. Used by permission of Tyndale House Publishers, Carol Stream, Illinois 60188. All rights reserved.

All emphasis in Scripture has been added.

Published in association with Stephanie Alton of the Blythe Daniel Agency, Inc.

Sections from chapter 3 were adapted from the book *I Can't Come Down* by Rachel G. Scott (Cleveland, OH: TKI Publishing, LLC, 2019), 21–25.

Edited by Amanda Cleary Eastep
Interior design: Brandi Davis
Cover design: Brittany Schrock
Author photo: Lauren Bethany Photography

Library of Congress Cataloging-in-Publication Data

Names: Scott, Rachel G., author.
Title: Taking the 5 leaps : experiencing God's faithfulness as you respond
   to his call / by Rachel G. Scott.
Other titles: Taking the five leaps
Description: Chicago, IL : Moody Publishers, 2024. | Includes
   bibliographical references. | Summary: "Rachel equips readers to go from
   delay to action. What kind of leap are you being invited to make? And
   how can you prepare, plan, and execute that leap? This book outlines
   five types of leaps you can take using illustrations from the Bible and
   personal stories"-- Provided by publisher.
Identifiers: LCCN 2023032756 | ISBN 9780802432025 (paperback) | ISBN
   9780802472854 (ebook)
Subjects: LCSH: Faith. | Trust in God--Christianity.
Classification: LCC BV4637 .S364 2024 | DDC 234/.23--dc23/eng/20231016
LC record available at https://lccn.loc.gov/2023032756

Originally delivered by fleets of horse-drawn wagons, the affordable paperbacks from D. L. Moody's publishing house resourced the church and served everyday people. Now, after more than 125 years of publishing and ministry, Moody Publishers' mission remains the same— even if our delivery systems have changed a bit. For more information on other books (and resources) created from a biblical perspective, go to www.moodypublishers.com or write to:

Moody Publishers
820 N. LaSalle Boulevard
Chicago, IL 60610

1 3 5 7 9 10 8 6 4 2

Printed in the United States of America

This book is dedicated to Willie, my amazing husband, who has believed in me since the day we met. Your love, faithfulness, and dedication have given me courage and freedom to dream BIG with God. You're my dream come true and the perfect leaping partner for me.

I Love You.

Contents

Introduction

One day, as I was mentoring a writer, the conversation shifted from talking about her writing to discussing the season of life she was currently navigating. She shared about the strong nudge she felt to transition from her secure career in the healthcare industry into her calling as a writer. I listened and watched her intensely as she explained what led her to this moment of awareness. As she talked, I could see the excitement, nervousness, concern, and uncertainty that accompanied her words.

She had a home, husband, and children. She knew she brought great value to the healthcare industry, both practically and spiritually. However, the time commitment it required in addition to family obligations left her unable to do what she felt passionate about and called to. She was ready for a change, but she didn't know how to go about it.

I knew the emotions and thoughts that she carried very well because that had been me almost two years prior. I ran from the nudging until I could no longer find peace or calm. Obedience, though risky, was my only escape. This woman, too, was processing if she was ready for that same risk. At the end of the conversation, we prayed, but I knew I didn't have answers for her. She was at a crossroads, and it seemed that her career was crippling her calling.

What I didn't know was that God was about to use that situation to transform my thinking and many others' mindsets as well.

After our discussion, I continued to think about her, the look on her face, the concern in her voice, and the tug on her heart. One day, I prayed and asked God two simple questions: "Is there only one way to go from a career to a calling?" and "Can You show me someone in the Bible who took leaps?"

"Can You show me someone in the Bible who . . . ?" has become one of my favorite questions to ask God. When I am confused, I have made it a habit to ask Him to show me someone in the Bible who has been through something similar, and I am always amazed at how quickly and accurately He shows me someone who fits the very scenario.

That question, and a listening ear to hear His response, is what became the catalyst for the Fisherman's Leap, Builder's Leap, Tentmaker's Leap, Shepherd's Leap, and Trailblazer's Leap—all of which I'm about to share with you in the pages of this book.

LET'S HAVE A SEAT

Let's pretend for a moment that you and I are sitting at your favorite coffee or tea spot. The noises surrounding us are the soft taps of the person in the corner typing away on his keyboard, the barista whipping together a beautiful cup of chai tea with coconut milk and cinnamon dolce syrup (that may just be my order), and gentle piano music playing in the background. It's the perfect setting for you to answer the questions I am about to ask:

"What did you dream of becoming when you were younger?"

"What do people always say you are good at?"

"What do people tell you they appreciate about you?"

"What are you naturally good at that you assume
everyone else already knows how to do?"

"How do you feel you have been called to serve God
and equip others in this season?"

After hearing your answers and engaging in a bit more discussion, I would help you to narrow down what you are most passionate about or feeling most called to *right now*. It's funny how we can help other people figure out their whole life and can barely figure out what to eat for dinner. I believe that's God's wise way of reminding us to never forget that we need each other.

Just remember, this moment of introspection isn't about what you don't know. Rather, it's about what you do know—and that's typically a lot more than we give ourselves credit for.

When I walk through a similar exercise with people I mentor, usually in the area of taking leaps, I often find that they are in one of three categories at any given point:

1. **Needing clarity**—knowing there is something greater they should be doing, but having no clue of what that something is.
2. **Needing direction**—knowing specifically what they should be doing, but being unsure of what to do next.
3. **Needing to take action**—knowing what to do and how to accomplish it, but for one reason or another, delaying taking the necessary steps.

These categories may change as we navigate different areas of life. As a parent, I may need some direction, but as a business owner, I may need to take action. As a spouse, I may need some clarity because—boy, oh boy—is there a lot to figure out here. But as an employee, I may need direction to better fulfill my employer's expectations for that role.

When it comes to taking leaps, having clarity and direction should prompt us to take action. Now, there are times when we may not have all the details. However, we often have enough information to take the next step, and that is what leaping is all about.

BEFORE WE BEGIN

I want you to think of that leap you are feeling called to make today. The following chapters will help you to determine what style of leaper you are and provide some simple ways you can prepare to take the specific leap you are feeling led to make.

At the end of the book, you will also find an appendix with a resource called "Scriptures to Stand On." This list of verses was created to help you meditate on truth and equip you for those moments when life and everything around you tell you to just stay where you are. You will find this to be an invaluable tool as you take leaps that are both big and small.

My dear friend, if you will allow me, I would love to be your leap coach for a few days, weeks, or months. We will go at your pace. I want to cheer you on as you learn from my mistakes and successes about how to leap into what God is calling you to do. Taking leaps always includes risks and tons of unknowns, but I want you to remember that the risk is worth the reward that comes with acting in obedience.

To begin our time together, I will be sharing some core concepts we must embrace in order to effectively and confidently take leaps. So, let's begin by first understanding the difference between a calling and a vision.

The Leaping Lifestyle

CHAPTER 1

From Calling to Vision

As my husband and I sat in the car outside of the financial adviser's office, tears streamed down my face. It was the first time since taking leaps from our jobs into full-time ministry that I'd cried this hard. The floodgates opened and, at the moment, no words of encouragement or Scripture would close them. These tears had been bottled up for weeks, if not months.

I often wonder what it feels like to be on the other end of my sudden tsunami of tears. This has only happened a few times in our marriage, and afterward, my husband always says that I caught him off guard. Quite honestly, I don't know when life will get so heavy, and I tend to hold it together for so long that my recourse will be a good ol' ugly cry.

But on that day, it was a dose of life with a dash of painful reality that became the icing on the cake.

My husband and I knew we were taking a huge leap of faith that most people would consider unwise if the details were known.

And that day, my thoughts were confirmed. As we sat at that long desk with the two cofounders of the financial planning company, one of them bombarded us with questions:

"What will you do when this money runs out?"

"You have a family to take care of. What will you do for their future?"

"This doesn't look like a sustainable plan."

"Why are you doing this?"

"What plans do you have next?"

"This isn't realistic."

The partner must have felt bad for us since she was the one who invited us to share more about our ministry and explore how they could support us. She tried to soften the blows by explaining how amazing the work was that we were embarking on and how many lives would be transformed, but her business partner wasn't hearing it. What he didn't know was that, as a calculated risk taker, I'd already considered everything the adviser was saying. I had questions, and I knew God had the answers. I was just waiting for Him to let me in on the details.

Any day now, God!

It's difficult to explain to people what you feel God told you in your secret place. It's called a secret for a reason. If He wanted everyone to know and understand, He'd call it "a public" place. Trying to logically explain something that you don't fully understand yourself is never easy. We didn't have all the details. We had just given God our yes, and yet that day, I felt like a complete lunatic.

As I exited the building on that hot summer afternoon, gripped with doubt, shame, and embarrassment, I started to wonder if we had heard God right.

AM I CRAZY?

Have you ever felt an undeniable nudge to do something completely outside of your comfort zone, but totally in the I-must-be-going-crazy zone?

Or have you been right in the place where you always dreamed you would be in a career with great potential for growth, income, and opportunity, only for you to get that feeling in your gut that you are not planted in the right garden?

These thoughts and feelings may be silent indicators of what I like to identify as your calling.

Our calling often presents itself through the unsettled feeling we have when what we are living to do isn't lining up with what we are longing to do. Or when we realize that we have a desire to aid in something far bigger than we have the capacity to understand. Ultimately, our calling reveals itself through a sudden or gradual awareness about a way that we can influence, impact, or transform a situation.

I think of the story of Samuel found in 1 Samuel 3 and how God called him into the role of a prophet. Three times God called Samuel's name. Finally, the third time, Samuel went to his teacher, Eli, who identified for him that it was God calling him and how to respond. What I find interesting is that Samuel didn't seem shocked the first two times that his name was called. He just assumed it was Eli. The tone of voice that called Samuel sounded familiar in a sense. Samuel was so used to listening to and obeying Eli, his default response put him in a place to hear the voice of God.

As you become aware of the voice of God, the beckoning you have been sensing will likely be presented through a tone that sounds familiar as well. Confirmation can occur through a sermon, podcast, online video, friend, or stranger. God will use whatever means He desires to get your attention as He calls you unto Himself.

But much like Samuel, you may not be comfortable with your calling, or you may not find it easy to respond (1 Sam. 3:15–18). It will require obedience and for you to surrender your will in exchange for God's way. It will require you to step into the unknown with the One who knows all.

However, God won't leave us completely unaware. Along the way, He reveals pieces of His plan, and He does that by turning the calling into a vision.

GOD, THE FIRST VISIONARY

Think of vision and calling as the answers to "what?" Vision answers "What is God showing you?" Calling answers "What is God asking of you right *now?*"

God knows how to impart His plans to each of us. He knows exactly how to share His agenda with His children. Through vision, we are given insight into His heavenly blueprint.

In Andy Stanley's book *Visioneering*, he discusses vision being associated with "the inability to accept things the way they are," and further explains that visionaries possess "a sense of conviction." This compulsion moves us "out of the realm of passive concern and into action."[1]

God was the first visionary.

This definition expresses the essence of why vision is important to taking the leap. God was the first visionary. He envisioned the world a certain way because that is the key to being a visionary. Each leap or action God leads us to take is one way His vision is birthed upon the earth.

God saw that the earth needed life. So, He created everything, including humanity. Because He created people with free will,

God also knew where their choices would eventually lead them. But He already had a plan in place; He had a vision to redeem what was broken because visionaries understand that sometimes we have to start with a clean slate.

How many things have you done and realized, *This isn't it—let me try this again?* Human beings' visions come with plans, but they don't always come with perfect plans that can't be disrupted by other factors.

My first adult hobby/business was a vision gone wrong. I had this great big plan to sell jewelry at a local mall. I put tons of hours into making dozens of earrings, only to find myself four hours into the day without a single customer or sale.

Back to the drawing board.

Or the time I sold credit card machines and thought that I'd build my own company from it, as the parent company assured me was possible. I spent hours driving to small businesses trying to convince them that they were missing out if they didn't have these new machines. Credit card machines would be the new way to sell products. As true as that may have been, trying to sell something new to people who liked the old way of doing things wasn't a lucrative endeavor. So, my dream to start a credit card machine sales company went down the drain when I didn't hit the sales quota.

Or the time I started a mentorship program for writers and had one semi-successful year, so I decided to do a full-out Black Friday sale with advertising and branding, only to fail in selling a single slot for the upcoming program. Guess where I went?

Back to the drawing board.

My friend, here is what I would like you to understand: when we are led by vision, we must be willing to make major changes along the way. Sometimes complete do-overs.

God's original plan was an earth that was filled with loving, righteous, blameless beings who walked in close fellowship with Him, much like Noah (see Gen. 6:9)—not corrupt, idol-worshiping, sinful humans, much like everyone else in the world.

He wanted a world that could live in the blessings He had reserved, not the curse it deserved.

Revelation 22:3–5 tells us:

> No longer will there be anything accursed, but the throne of God and of the Lamb will be in it, and his servants will worship him. They will see his face, and his name will be on their foreheads. And night will be no more. They will need no light of lamp or sun, for the Lord God will be their light, and they will reign forever and ever.

God is the ultimate definition of a visionary. He wrote a plan to save the world and shared it with us in His Word. Currently, we are seeing the pieces of His strategic plan in motion all around us. He sees where our world is headed. He has a glorious and suitable way to solve the problem of sin that is destroying the place He created for us, His children, to occupy. He desires to fix it, but He desires our partnership along the way. We partner best with God in two ways: prayer and execution.

HEAVEN'S REWARD

Our partnership with Christ's vision makes us visionaries, and as visionaries in Christ, we bring solutions to the world's problems. People with problems recognize those who can help solve them. This is why so many ran to Jesus when they saw Him. They may not have known how, but somehow, they knew He was a solution to the problems in *their* world. When we become followers of Jesus, we become a solution to the problems that exist in this world, and people will come from far and wide just to seek the insight that we have by way of heavenly wisdom. Our access to this divine wisdom, knowledge, and understanding is truly priceless. Jesus modeled this for us very well.

However, as you give God your yes, you will find many emotions—fear, excitement, anxiety, frustration, and many more—knocking at the door of your heart. But remember, we shouldn't let them lead. Emotions are great servants but terrible masters, especially if they are rooted in lies.

Lies will say,

"It will be too hard."

"It will become a financial burden."

"It will not line up with future plans that have been on your heart."

"You can't do it now because . . ."

"You have to know the end at the beginning."

"God taking care of you may look like suffering."

When you begin to feel these emotions while partnering with God in taking the leap, it's an indication to make an exchange—the lie that the enemy wants you to obsess over for the truth that God wants you to meditate on. Remind yourself, *The risk is worth heaven's reward.*

When this happens, it's also a great time to read the Scriptures to Stand On aloud that have been provided to you at the end of this book and keep your eyes on Jesus. As we begin to take this journey, I want to remind you, "The blessing of the LORD makes rich, and he adds no sorrow with it" (Prov. 10:22).

Whatever you choose in obedience to God will not harm you. It will work out well for you as you begin to declare with expectation what Romans 8:28 exhorts: this will turn out for my good.

We are not called to figure out how to solve problems; we are called to face them. God already has the solution. He just needs someone who is willing to stand in the gap between earth and heaven. Later we will discuss the power of prayer as you take your leap, but know this: prayer is key to progressing as a visionary. Visionaries must replace their fear with prayer so that God's wisdom and insight can be accessed. This means not leaning on our own understanding of what the vision could be saying but rather asking God for His interpretation and revelation.

Prayer is our greatest preparation. The work we do in the secret place to hear God's heart and voice will prepare us for the work He has called us to do openly. The secret place, as I have come to know it, is the place where the scrolls of heaven are revealed to us so that we can get strategy and wisdom from the throne of grace. It's where we could learn to hear and steward the heart of God for His people. It's where we may get our marching orders and weaponry for the work ahead. It is where the strategy for the vision is unveiled.

There will always be a war going on among our spirit, soul, and flesh. The flesh desires comfort and convenience; the soul desires security and certainty. Yet, when we have chosen Christ, we are filled with the Holy Spirit, and the Holy Spirit desires the will of God. It would be great if all three of them were always in sync, but often they are not. However, there is one authority who can balance them all when we are surrendered: God. He can bring peace where chaos may try to exist. And through prayer, we access the Holy Spirit who then "intercedes for us with groanings too deep for words" (Rom. 8:26).

And the beauty of the secret place is that it is found when we silence the noise around us and allow ourselves to tune in to the peace beyond our understanding that God provides.

TOO BIG FOR ME

God led Abraham into new territory, Peter into ministry, Nehemiah into a new industry, Paul into new leadership, and Jesus into a new level of honor. And He is calling us into a new encounter with Him through our leaps.

The call may be great, but the crown will be greater.

To say that God was the first visionary can feel a bit intimidating, especially when we consider that He is calling us to partner in that vision.

Often when people become crippled by fear of the unknown, it's because they begin formulating ideas and possibilities for what it may look like if they partner with God's big vision. I always say that the enemy works in three ways: imagination, speculation, and negative thoughts.

He will try to get us to imagine ourselves living out the worst-case scenario of what we will sacrifice as we pursue the vision. Then he uses evidence from the past to try to form a false narrative in our minds of what *could* happen based on what has happened to us or others who did this same thing. Finally, if the first two tricks don't work, he just whispers negative thoughts, lies, doubts, and threats. He will say anything to get us to believe that God doesn't have our best interest at heart with His request.

But that will no longer work for us because we will choose to trust God's wisdom, truth, and best for our lives, even if what He asks is out of our comfort zone. Remember the Bible instructs: "And everyone who has left houses or brothers or sisters or father or mother or children or lands, for my name's sake, will receive a hundredfold and will inherit eternal life" (Matt. 19:29).

What is this saying? It implies that anybody willing to leave their comfort zone—which is what a home represents—and follow

Jesus will receive much more than they lost. He is giving us a beautiful promise as we surrender in obedience.

We may be asked to make a big sacrifice, but it's not too big for the God who will carry the load with you. God will put His super on your natural and help you walk out His great vision.

I've heard it said that we are not building our kingdom; we are building God's and He knows just how to build His kingdom well.

CHAPTER 2

The Vehicle of a Vision

Hannah Hurnard, the author of *Hinds' Feet on High Places*, takes us on a journey of being led by God into His greater plan for our lives. As the main character Much-Afraid learns to exchange comfort for courage, we get to see how she overcomes the many obstacles that block her from becoming the person God created her to be.

At the beginning of the book, Much-Afraid begins to share with the Chief Shepherd her desire and hesitancy with regard to traveling to High Places: "These mountains are so steep and dangerous. I have been told that only the hinds and the deer can move on them safely."

In response, the Chief Shepherd tells her:

"It is quite true that the way up to the High Places is both difficult and dangerous. . . . It has to be, so that nothing which is an enemy of Love can make the ascent and invade the Kingdom. Nothing blemished or in any way imperfect is allowed there, and the inhabitants of the High Places do need 'hinds' feet.' I have them myself . . . and like a young hart or a roebuck I can go leaping on the mountains and skipping on the hills with the greatest ease and pleasure."[2]

Why am I sharing this with you?

As I begin to explain the five types of leaps and the story behind each one, it may be tempting to imagine the dangers that could lie ahead of you. However, I want to remind you that leaping is far less about making it to the peak and far more about who you become in the process. It is about ascending to the high place, not descending into defeat. This is what Much-Afraid learned as she traveled and what we will learn as well.

A leap is a vehicle that God uses to move us from preparing to planning and eventually to executing the vision He has given us. These three steps—Preparing, Planning, and Executing—are what I like to call heaven's PPE.

PREPARE, PLAN, EXECUTE

Years ago, I had an acquaintance who I would meet up with occasionally. She was motivated, focused, and had her entire life planned out. Whenever we'd get together, I would listen as she talked about finishing school and landing her dream job, which would lead to fulfilling all her subsequent life plans. Each year's plan included a milestone, from starting her career and getting married to having children (in a specific order), and everything in between.

I would often listen to her while wondering to myself, *What if it doesn't work out that way? She will be devastated.* One day, I asked her that exact question. "What if it doesn't happen as you planned?" Her response was simple (and obvious to her). "It will," she said, looking at me as if I were from another planet. I conceded and moved on to another conversation. Honestly, I couldn't argue against her confidence.

Needless to say, things turned out completely different than she had ever planned. Unexpected losses led her down a path that she never dreamed of. Looking back, I couldn't fault her for planning the way she had. We had learned to do just that. I'm sure, like me, she had been taught the old adage, "If you fail to plan, you plan to fail."

I don't recall the first person who said those words to me, but from that moment until now, it's stuck with me. She had obviously heard the same thing. And in many ways, this thinking is beneficial in business, parenting, time management, and life. Success is about how we plan, prepare, and execute, in that exact order.

However, I noticed something unique about how the kingdom of God operates. In the kingdom, instead of *planning* first, God starts our journey off by *preparing* us. God tends to prepare us initially through experiences that become lessons. Then when He reveals the plans He had all along, we are able to execute them based on the knowledge we gained during the prior preparation season.

Understanding how that one small change, preparation *before* the planning, works in real-time will make all the difference as we begin to learn about making leaps.

WHAT LEAP ARE YOU TAKING?

As we begin to discuss the leaps, keep in mind there are two ways to look at these leaps: your natural inclination (which leap you tend to do most often, naturally) and your situational need (which leap you are feeling called to make currently).

For example, the Fisherman's Leap comes naturally to me because I'm always looking for new and fresh opportunities. However, the Shepherd's Leap is a little harder for me since I like stability and routine in my home life.

Understanding both our natural inclination (or predisposition) and our situational need with regard to leaps helps us respond and adjust quicker. When we are aware of these two things, we don't spend as much time questioning our choices or God's leading. We respond faster because we understand and acknowledge the way God has wired us or what He is leading us to do, and trust that they are both part of His divine will.

I've created an online quiz to help you identify the natural inclination you have as a leaper. (You can take this quiz by visiting rachelgscott.com/takingthe5leapsquiz.) Our time together in this book will focus more on your situational needs, yet the tools you learn will give you the knowledge and understanding needed for both scenarios.

The Fisherman's Leap

I've always wanted to experience the world of fishing. Over the years, I imagined myself on a 73-degree summer day, sitting on a still boat in the middle of a calm lake, waves lapping against the hull. The idea of having nothing around but beautiful water, blue skies, and perfect rays of sun seems heavenly. Yet, my dream fishing trip comes to a screeching halt when the sound of my two teenagers arguing from the other room reminds me that I am not on anyone's boat in the middle of calm water on a perfect 73-degree day!

That image of fishing is perfect for today's leisure pastime, but nothing compared to the disciples' lives as fishermen.

The career of a fisherman in the Bible was not one that was admired or esteemed. It required long, hard hours of work with little to no return. Fishermen were far from the elite class, but their work was a fundamental part of the economic system of that time in biblical history. Not only did they have to patiently wait for fish, but they also had to sort them for sale, wash and mend nets, and complete other tedious yet essential tasks.

Fishermen, such as Peter, Andrew, James, and John, were hardworking business owners and good at what they did! Through their efforts, they established financial security for their families. However, perhaps right at the height of fishing season, a life-changing moment occurred. They were faced with an ultimatum: eternal life or earthly rewards.

Were they willing to give up all they had built and their legacies to follow Jesus?

This is the path of the Fisherman's Leap. The person who makes this leap has been called to leave his or her career and go fully into something else God has instructed them to do. Essentially, **this leap is to walk away from the known and travel into the unknown.**

Although each of the disciples was called to follow Jesus and leave everything, we learn that the plan Jesus had for Peter was distinct. This is why we will focus primarily on Peter's story when talking about the Fisherman's Leap moving forward.

Here is the thing—in the end, Peter had to make a decision that we all must make at some point, no matter the leap. Are we willing to deny, pick up, and follow (Matt. 16:24)? Peter chose to follow; what will you choose?

The Tentmaker's Leap

One of the first ministries my husband and I started was in 2016 while we were still working full-time and raising a house full of children. We certainly already had a full plate, but we still felt

God nudging us to step out and start a ministry that would serve blended families around the globe.

For several years, we worked full-time during the day and, in the evening or on the weekends, we planned events, created content, shared on podcasts or television interviews, managed blog contributors, conducted workshops, and more.

Doing this was not an easy undertaking! It was a season when our willingness to say yes to God wasn't contingent on convenience, but rather obedience.

Looking back, I realize that juggling full-time work, family, and ministry was what we had been called to do for that season. God equips those He calls, and He did that with us just as He did with the apostle Paul.

Paul was skilled in what we would now call apologetics and tentmaking. His knowledge of religion and Jewish law worked as a disadvantage to followers of the risen Christ until his conversion on the road to Damascus. Once Paul was converted to Christianity, his focus became the transformation and salvation of the Gentiles, but he still had to have a profession or trade to obtain income. As we see in Acts 20:34, his tentmaking funded his ministry and personal needs so that he could focus on instruction for the church.

The person who has a similar experience is known as the Tentmaker. Much like how Paul used his skill to build tents to support himself and the ministry, the person in this leap is fulfilling the work of God all while God blesses the work of his or her hands through their career.

Being a tentmaker requires stepping out and partnering with God as your job and God's calling occupy space in the same season. It also requires a strong community, willingness to delegate, and trust in God for the details, as we see with Paul. He always ends his letters by thanking those who are co-laboring with him because the work of a tentmaker cannot be done alone.

The Builder's Leap

Nehemiah is one of my favorite characters in the Bible. I have always admired his ability to stay focused and combat distractions in order to complete the work God called him to do. His understanding of the temporary nature of his assignment and leadership ability are both impressive and encouraging.

The Bible tells us that Nehemiah was a high-ranking official in the Persian court of King Artaxerxes I at the capital city of Susa and was a cupbearer to the king. He was asked to travel nearly a thousand miles to rebuild and reestablish a community that had been destroyed for decades, and he accomplished this assignment in just fifty-two days (Neh. 6:15).

Nehemiah's task of rebuilding the wall was not planned. The first chapter of the book of Nehemiah explains that his life was interrupted by a visit from his brother and men from Judah who had come with news that "the remnant there in the province who had survived the exile is in great trouble and shame. The wall of Jerusalem is broken down, and its gates are destroyed by fire" (Neh. 1:3).

After much prayer and petition, Nehemiah was sent on a temporary assignment to rebuild the walls of Jerusalem to help fortify the city. How do we know it was temporary? In Nehemiah 2:6, it says, "The king said to me (the queen sitting beside him), 'How long will you be gone, and when will you return?' So it pleased the king to send me when I had given him a time."

Nehemiah's leap was not the same as Peter's or Paul's. Nehemiah's leap is what I aptly call the Builder's Leap.

This leap is one in which you are temporarily called away from a full-time career to fulfill God's work in other ways, but you will return to the career in some capacity or to any area of work once the task is complete.

Nehemiah was on a specific assignment and when that assignment was complete, he was to return to being a cupbearer for the king. He put everything in place financially and logistically to step away from his work with the understanding that he would be returning.

I hope that this will be freeing for you if you feel called to take a leap to care for an elderly parent, homeschool a child, start a business, write a book, or anything else that may actually be a temporary assignment.

Allow God to reveal His plans to you and trust Him with the next steps.

The Shepherd's Leap

There's nothing better to me than beautiful palm trees, sunny blue skies, summer dresses, and flip-flops. Unfortunately, the location where I currently live boasts gray clouds, snow boots, coats, and gloves 65 percent of the year.

Recently, the topic of living in a warmer climate has been at the top of my list. My husband agrees that the conditions would be much more accommodating for us and our family, and since we both work from home, career flexibility would help. Yet, there are many things to consider that aren't quite as simple.

Will we sell or rent our home? Is the market good? Where will we live? Will the new school system be good for our children? Who will care for our elderly parents? What if the market in our industry changes? What if we don't go, and then live with the regret that we didn't?

The list goes on and on.

The unknown is risky and can be scary no matter how many answers we may have at our disposal. Wisdom and worry can be difficult to distinguish between in moments like this. Relocation is a huge leap, and it's the one God called Abraham to take. This leap, known as the Shepherd's Leap, is centered around Abraham, a shepherd who was called to relocate with his family and wealth (see Gen. 12:5) to occupy new territory.

In Genesis 12:1, God tells Abraham to "go from your country and your kindred and your father's house to the land that I will show you." If we don't read what happened before this, it can be very easy to misinterpret what God was telling Abraham.

In Genesis 11:27–32, we find the story of Abraham's father, Terah, who began a mission with his son and grandson Lot to leave the land of Ur of the Chaldeans and set out to the land of Canaan. However, in verse 31, we learn that "when they came to Haran, they settled there," and the family remained there until Terah died.

Later, the Word tells us that Abraham finally made it to Canaan (see Gen. 12:5). Wait, pause. Often, we think Abraham didn't know where he was going. That is not at all the case. Abraham was not aimlessly traveling, waiting for God to tell him when to pitch his tent, but rather intentionally journeying so that he could complete the last instructions that the generation before him had left unfinished. It was in Canaan that God could fulfill His promise to His people through Abraham. But Abraham had to be in the location where the land could be shown to him.

I have often heard people refer to this Scripture as a reason to take a leap without direction, clarity, or resources. "Well, God didn't tell *Abraham* where to go," they say. Before I knew better, I personally used this as a reason for leaps and found myself in a mess. If we don't understand that Abraham had provisions and knew where he was going, we may use this Scripture to inaccurately validate our lack of preparedness. Abraham was being called to new territory in order to complete an assignment that his father had left incomplete. God gave him all the provisions he needed ahead of time so that he had no reason to delay.

The Shepherd's Leap is about going into new territory for something God wants to release to us. It's about being entrusted with more because God has promises that can only be fulfilled in that place. If you are being called to the Shepherd's Leap, know that you get to be the generation that walks in obedience and goes from the pitstop into His purpose.

The Trailblazer's Leap

When we think of all the leaps we make throughout our lifetime, it might help to know that our model and the greatest example of living a leaping lifestyle is Jesus!

That's why He is our example for the Trailblazer's Leap.

You see, Jesus went before us in all things, and that includes taking leaps. He modeled for us what it looks like to live and lead a lifestyle of leaps. Although He said that we will do greater works than He did (John 14:12), His leap will always remain the greatest to ever be done. This is why His leap is called the Trailblazer's Leap. Because He did it first, His children can experience it in an even greater capacity than we otherwise might!

Here is what I mean.

John 3:13 tells us, "No one has ascended into heaven except he who descended from heaven, the Son of Man." Here we see Jesus exchanging His seat in heavenly places at the right hand of the Father for a temporary assignment that required Him to occupy new territory on earth. His choice to go from heaven to earth models for us the Shepherd's Leap and the temporary nature of this leap models for us the Builder's Leap.

When He came to dwell among us as Savior of the world, carpenter, and teacher, He performed both ministry and career duties. Both roles and responsibilities occupied space in the same season until He went into full-time public ministry. All of this is a beautiful example of what it looks like to take the Tentmaker's Leap.

And we dare not forget about the final three years of Jesus' life where He fully committed Himself to the work of the Father through full-time ministry. Up until this time, He honored His parents by working in the family business as a carpenter and spent time learning in the synagogues. Any ministry work He did was to be kept private as was His divine mission on the earth. But at the age of thirty, He separated Himself from the family business to begin His full-time ministry. This, my friend, is exactly what it looks like to take the Fisherman's Leap.

If you are someone who has taken all of the other leaps, you are now a trailblazer. You get to teach and support others as they take leaps. This doesn't mean that your leaping days are over. It just means you have a little more skin in the game than someone who hasn't made leaps before.

Leaping isn't for the faint of heart, but if we understand that it's so much bigger than us, we won't grow weary in well-doing.

Friend, leaping is a lifestyle. That doesn't make it easy, but it is a reality. As you read this book, I want you to consider how many leaps you have taken in your lifetime. Think about parents or friends who have taken leaps. You will begin to see a pattern. It's a common part of our journey here on earth, but God equips us in the most unimaginable ways.

So, what are leaps really about?

I'm glad you asked.

CHAPTER 3

The Purpose of It All

W hat am I here for?"

"What is my purpose?"

"Why am I here?"

I've heard these questions asked many times. Conversations, sermons, videos, books, and movies have all been dedicated to finding the answers. These questions plague the thoughts of every human being at some point, and if they go unanswered, we will find ourselves lost and feeling that we don't belong.

If we are deeply pondering our purpose, it is often because we want to know why we exist and what we should be doing with our existence. It's an indication that we feel limited by our current situation, and we are not living fully in light of all we know we can contribute to the people, places, and things around us. These questions are usually posed by someone who is ready for more, and they find themselves at a crossroads in life.

When we attempt to answer this, it's important to obtain wisdom from God. How do I know this? Because in Psalm 33:11 we see that God—in His infinite love, faithfulness, and wisdom—makes clear that "the counsel of the LORD stands forever, the plans of his heart to all generations."

If God already knows the plans, wouldn't He know the purpose of those plans as well?

Something I've observed over time is that "Why am I here?" doesn't always mean "Why am I alive?" There are times when it means, "What am I supposed to be doing in this current season or moment in my life?" "What am I supposed to be doing so I can be most productive as a mother, father, husband, wife, son, daughter, employee, business owner, church member, or whatever role I find myself in?" These thoughts tend to reveal unfulfillment rather than uncertainty but at times can mean a bit of both.

In order to truly explore these questions, we must first define the distinct difference between two words: "purpose" and "assignment."

PURPOSE VS. ASSIGNMENT

Purpose is defined as "an intention or aim; a reason for doing something or for allowing something to happen."[1]

The similar word for *assignment* means "the state or fact of being chosen for a position or duty."[2]

These two words, although seemingly similar, are distinctly different. Our assignments are the ways in which God wants to use the gifts He has placed in us for His glory within the world and the role He has called us to play in a specific time or season. God gives us these assignments, or appoints us, so that He can fulfill His purpose through us. Think of it this way: purpose is the "why," and assignment is the "how." Why is God asking you to do this, and how are you going to do it?

And what if I told you that we have all been given the *same* purpose?

Matthew 28:18–20 says, "And Jesus came and said to them, 'All authority in heaven and on earth has been given to me. Go therefore and make disciples of all nations, baptizing them in the name of the Father and of the Son and of the Holy Spirit, teaching them to observe all that I have commanded you. And behold, I am with you always, to the end of the age.'"

> Assignments are defined by the purpose, and the purpose is fulfilled through the assignments.

Our purpose is now defined by Jesus' command. We are to walk in all the authority that has been given to us on earth and in heaven (see Ps. 8 and Heb. 1) and make disciples of nations. This is the reason we exist: to make His name known throughout the earth. This is our why! Assignments are defined by the purpose, and the purpose is fulfilled through the assignments.

By spreading the message of belief in Jesus Christ and bringing people into the knowledge of Him, we walk fully in the purpose for which we have been created because it is through the message of Jesus that hope is found and salvation is accessible.

We can hope in many things, but it is only hope in Jesus Christ that leads us to eternal life!

If you have found yourself in a season of wondering *What now?* or *What next?*, allow me to take a moment and reassure you that your time spent with God will reveal more to you than any book, sermon, or social media app ever could. He defines how our assignments support our roles in His purpose and plan. So, we have to be attentive to Him like a student is to a teacher. We cannot learn this outside of intimacy, relationship, and time with the One who carries the blueprint.

In His blueprints, God has all the answers and tools we will need to succeed in our assignments. He already knows the answers to the who, what, when, where, why, and how. It looks kind of like this:

Who: You and God
What: Your Assignment
When: The Appointed Time
Where: Your Heart
Why: The harvest is plentiful, but the workers are few
　　(see Luke 10:2)
How: Taking LEAPS of faith

I know that right now may not be the most ideal time to fulfill that assignment by taking a leap, but if God is leading you to it, then it's the appointed time, which means it's the perfect time. We will talk more about this in a later chapter, but for now, just know timing is God's specialty.

WHEN PURPOSE AND ASSIGNMENT LOCK ARMS

I remember when I felt led to start a blended family ministry, one of my first ministry endeavors. I'd grown up in a blended family, so I was fully aware of the various challenges of being part of one. All families have challenges, but blended families face unique ones. Being the youngest in my family, I was hit hardest by those challenges. I never had the opportunity to experience a single holiday, birthday, or event with all my siblings present.

Small but significant encounters such as this became motivating factors in my development of an organization to support others, especially after my husband and I got married and became a blended family. The vision was birthed from a life I had not seen but knew was possible. So that ministry became the assignment. And when my husband came on board with me, it took wings of its own. Starting an organization was a very bold move for my husband and me because many would say we didn't have enough experience to talk about the dynamics of this special family makeup yet.

Though that may have been true, we did have wisdom that we received from those who already walked the journey, as well as revelation from God on how He wanted us to blend. That was enough for us to start. As we moved forward, we began to realize that people weren't looking for someone with a perfect story. They were looking for someone who was walking the journey with them and would be bold enough to talk about it. We were that couple.

There is nothing more amazing than when a heavenly assignment meets the human vessel God has created to deliver it to the world. It's such an honor to watch the pieces come together and observe the story as it unfolds. When assignment and purpose lock arms, it's not about what you can do on your own; it's about what God can do through you. All He needs is your yes and a willingness to be obedient to the assignments He puts before you.

THE GREAT SACRIFICE

With billions of people on the planet and new babies being born by the second, I think it's safe to say that whatever your assignment is, the impact has the potential to be bigger than you could ever imagine. There are no insignificant assignments within the kingdom of God. Every assignment is significant in fulfilling *the* greater purpose.

You may say, "I am a homeschool mom. All I do is teach and clean." I would remind you that your contribution to your children's lives will have a lifelong, generational impact.

You may feel, "I am just an employee at a dead-end job, and all I do is sit in a cubicle all day," but I would suggest that no assignment is a dead end. It's simply a place where your impact and influence look different. Your contribution to the atmosphere of that place of employment is important. You are making an impact.

You may believe, "I am just a grandparent. I never went to school or completed my degree," and I would gently respond and say, "Wisdom comes from God and your grandchild and children need that wisdom, love, and support more than anyone else on this planet. No one else can give them what should be poured into them from you. Your words and time are making an impact."

You may think, "I am so tired of being single. All of my friends are getting married and having children, and I am sitting here alone." I would reply, "Someone is watching how you wait. Someone is looking at your journey of singleness and learning how to serve God in their season of singleness. You are making an impact."

Remember, every assignment that God gives us is a contribution to His greater purpose. The key words here are *God gives us*. The ones we give ourselves will not have the same outcome.

Learning to be okay with the season of the assignment that we are in will become our lifeline:

. . . When we see moms on vacation because they seem to have the time and finances to travel with their children, or when we see people working their dream jobs, and it looks like they are living their best life because of it.

. . . When we see grandparents spending time with friends and getting to live free from the responsibility of supporting their children and grandchildren, or when we see women getting married and cuddling with their husbands while we choose to use our time of singleness to draw closer to God.

Remember, our assignments will often require a sacrifice or exchange of our will for God's. To be entrusted with a heavenly assignment is a great honor and has unimaginable reward.

PURPOSE NOT PUNISHMENT

Our view of God will define how we value the assignment He has given us and our commitment to accomplishing it through obedient leaps.

As I was transitioning from being a full-time teacher into full-time entrepreneur, I was terrified. Everything around me seemed to say, "Don't do it! This is crazy!" It was the risk of a lifetime, and the unknowns were limitless. But here is what a sister in Christ told me one day during a breakfast meetup: "Rachel, God will not punish you for your obedience." Those words were like a wave of calm to my turbulent soul.

When she said this to me, I felt myself release the breath I had been unknowingly holding for months. Those words became the words I lived by and still live by as I walk out into the many unknowns of being a writer and entrepreneur. When we choose purpose, we are choosing the unknown, unfamiliar, uncomfortable, and the center of God's will. This is right where He wants us to be. It is a place of beautiful encounter where promises are kept, dying to self occurs, and freedom is available to be all He has called us to become.

A hard truth that was uncovered during this part of the journey was that I had been living as if I were an orphan child without a heavenly Father. I was one of those people who always needed a backup plan in case God didn't come through. These, as well as many other trust issues, were greatly impacting my ability to see God's hand of provision and heart for me as His daughter. It was as if I believed God was going to fall asleep on the job. The painful reality was that my relationship with God was severely limited by my distorted view of Him, and as a result, I struggled to operate in the immediate obedience that God required of me.

God knew this needed to be addressed before I could continue taking leaps with Him because leaps instructed by God can't be led by lies.

There was no way I could walk in God's purpose with a broken view of Him. I had to work on not allowing brokenness to be the lens through which I saw, identified, and engaged with my perfect heavenly Father.

As I took the time to learn the nature of God—through worship and time spent in His Word, prayer, and devotion—He began to heal me of past and present wounds that had led to a lack of trust in His nature and faithfulness. This process, although difficult, was worth it.

Why is our view of God so important to purpose? A tainted view of God compromises the assignment and gives the enemy room to contradict God's purpose. It allows the enemy input on what should only be accessible to God and His master plan for our lives. When the enemy gets access to those things, his mission is to steal, kill, or destroy the vision (John 10:10). This is exactly what happened in the garden of Eden with Eve. The serpent tainted Eve's view of God, which led to more pain and suffering than she could have ever imagined (Gen. 3).

A proper view of God is one led by truth about His nature and love for His children: you and me.

As you walk out the purpose, remember that it is God whose

purpose defines the direction your life should go. We are working for His "well done," and as we work together in fulfilling the purpose, His kingdom is expanded, heaven is exploding, and He is being glorified.

The Bible says, "For we are his workmanship, created in Christ Jesus for good works, which God prepared beforehand, that we should walk in them" (Eph. 2:10).

He knows how we are going to fulfill that good work which He has prepared. We just have to say yes so our assignment can begin.

And it will often begin with a leap!

ONE LAST THOUGHT

You don't have to be perfect to walk in purpose.

I am a recovering perfectionist. Looking back at my life, I realize that perfectionism made its grand entrance into my life after my parents' divorce. It was then that I found myself trying to keep the pieces of my young, rattled life together by excelling in academics, band, music, and school clubs. Perfectionism stayed around in adulthood and through the experiences of having a child out of wedlock, a failed marriage, and remarriage. It was not until I began to see the negative impact it had on my life as a wife and mother that I began to walk the journey of healing. Quite honestly, I used to wear perfectionism like a badge of honor until it wore me down. Unfortunately, I had no idea how to combat this because it had been part of my life for so long.

I believe that people become perfectionistic, critical, lazy, irrational, pessimistic, passive, aggressive, greedy, selfish—and the list continues—because that is how they learned

> God can do more with our willingness than He could ever do with our worthiness.

to adapt to life. Before, I thought it was more important for things to look like they were under control than for them to actually be under control.

However, after learning more about God and His nature, I can confidently say that God doesn't call any of us to these assignments because we are qualified or perfect. It's not about our ability to do it outside of Him. He knows what we can and can't do. It's about our willingness to be obedient. God can do more with our willingness than He could ever do with our worthiness.

He is trusting you to fulfill your assignment, not because you are perfect, but because He knows that if you choose obedience, He can—and will—handle the rest.

CHAPTER 4

The Setup

One of my favorite verses in the Bible comes from the book of Romans: "And we know that for those who love God all things work together for good, for those who are called according to his purpose" (Rom. 8:28).

How refreshing. Yet, if I can be honest, when leaping, I didn't anticipate the *working together* part to take so long.

Here's how it went in my mind:

1. I'd say yes to what God called me to do.
2. The next *new* thing would be staring me right in the face (no figuring out what to do or waiting for it to happen).
3. Then, God would send me a sign or person to facilitate the advancement of the new thing so the process could move quickly.
4. I'd experience the same success or greater in the new assignment as I had with the old one.
5. God would get the glory from the story, and I would get the satisfaction of knowing that I obeyed Him.

Simple enough, right?

In no way was I prepared for how it actually went. Many of the bumps, bruises, and setbacks that occurred along the way shocked me at first.

I'd wonder to myself, *If God loves me and told me to take this step, why is it so difficult?*

He does love me, and He did tell me, but I once heard someone say, "Simple doesn't always mean easy."

The undesirable truth is that with each leap we're taught new lessons presented in the form of challenges or difficulties. To my surprise, these challenges were actually intended to build my spiritual muscle and tenacity for the assignment I'd been given and the blessings connected to it.

I believe that the bigger the battle, the bigger the blessing, and this has proven to be true in my life as well as in other fellow believers in Christ, such as Steven Adjei.

Recently, I interviewed Steven, who is the author of *Pay the Price*, on my *Taking the Leaps* podcast. During our time together, he shared details about his ten-year journey after leaping into entrepreneurship. He expressed how he lost his sister, declared bankruptcy after a bad business deal, and practically lost his family trying to pursue his entrepreneurial dream. Eventually, he hit his rock bottom and was ready to quit.

> **God doesn't get the glory out of any story; He gets the glory out of His story.**

As I listened to him speak, I began to feel many familiar emotions. Grief, guilt, and fear were unwelcomed but very present companions during that season of his life, and I'd been there myself.

But right when he was due to return from his sister's funeral, he met a woman who expressed a desire to partner with him in his business endeavors. Hesitantly, he leaned into the opportunity. It was that partnership during one of the darkest seasons of his life that led to his first big million-dollar deal, a month after his sister's death.[1]

Steven's story has pain and purpose written all over it. However, through his hardships, we are awakened to a simple yet profound truth about the nature of God that I've come to realize: God doesn't get the glory out of any story; He gets the glory out of His story.

Although we all have a version of our life story that we want to live, it's in the realm of God's sovereign will that He can get the glory from our story. And the greatest news is that when we find ourselves overwhelmed with the leap, God is faithful. He will take care of everything that concerns us, just like He did with Steven.

WORTH THE WAIT

The coming of Jesus was the greatest moment in history, and yet even this life-changing moment came after a season of waiting.

Since the fall, we've needed a Savior. Satan intended to destroy anyone and anything made in the image of God (see Revelation 12), and death was the only way to make that possible. His deception in the garden of Eden introduced Adam and Eve to a world of sin and death.

In short, the fall became the catalyst for a dreadful future on this side of heaven. A future that included pain, suffering, and separation from our heavenly Father. After that moment, our only hope of restoration was the intervention of a loving Savior who would free us from the bondage of sin. Jesus' arrival into the world led to the victory we would need for reconciliation to God.

But this didn't happen overnight. Some theologians believe the span between Adam's sin and Jesus' arrival was close to five thousand years.[2]

So, what happened between what *was* and what *needed* to be?

Well, the entire Old Testament reveals this, but when we come to the book of Matthew in the New Testament, we are met with a key *before Christ* moment that set the stage for our redemption story. Here we meet John the Baptist, the cousin of Jesus and son of Zechariah, whom God called to lead the charge in preparation for His Son and our Savior. Just as with Jesus' coming, John's birth fulfilled the prophecy given centuries before his arrival. Both Isaiah and Malachi speak prophetically about this moment in biblical history.

Isaiah says,

A voice cries:
"In the wilderness prepare the way of the LORD;
    make straight in the desert a highway for our God.
Every valley shall be lifted up,
    and every mountain and hill be made low;
the uneven ground shall become level,
    and the rough places a plain.
And the glory of the LORD shall be revealed,
    and all flesh shall see it together,
        for the mouth of the LORD has spoken." (Isa. 40:3–5)

Malachi follows with these words,

"Behold, I send my messenger, and he will prepare the way before me. And the Lord whom you seek will suddenly come to his temple; and the messenger of the covenant in whom you delight, behold, he is coming, says the LORD of hosts." (Mal. 3:1)

John the Baptist was called from the womb and spent his entire life preparing for Jesus to come and remove the sins of the world. He understood that our communion with God was contingent upon our right standing with Him. John's message of repentance saved many, but it angered even more. Yet, he was dedicated to his assignment unto death.

Near the end of John's life, while imprisoned for preaching repentance, his disciples went to the jail and began to tell him about the marvelous works of a man named Jesus. It was at that moment that John asks his disciples to deliver this message to Jesus spoken in Matthew 11:3, "Are you the one who is to come, or shall we look for another?"

This was a simple yet necessary question. But why would he ask this question, especially after being the one to baptize Jesus and proclaim Him as the Messiah?

Let's consider the cultural reality of that time in history. During this period, as is also true today, many people engaged in practices that contradicted biblical values. Things such as idolatry, mythology, and sorcery were common religious beliefs and practices at that time. John, like any good leader, may have been protecting his disciples from possibly being led astray by false teachers. He could have messed up in assuming Jesus was the Messiah because if He was, wouldn't He save John from his suffering? John also understood the assignment he had been given, so perhaps he didn't want to risk releasing his responsibility into the wrong person's hands. He was willing to endure until the end of his days, once he knew that he hadn't missed the mark.

The Moody Bible Commentary explains it this way:

> John's question . . . is understandable in light of his own prophesying about the Messiah coming with judgment ([Matt.] 3:7–12),

but there was little judgment so far in His ministry. In addition, most of the Jewish people anticipated a Messiah who would come as a great warrior king like David to free Israel from her oppressors.[3]

Jesus' response let John know that the wait for the coming Messiah was over and well worth it. "And Jesus answered them, 'Go and tell John what you hear and see: the blind receive their sight and the lame walk, lepers are cleansed and the deaf hear, and the dead are raised up, and the poor have good news preached to them'" (Matt. 11:4–5).

In verses 10 and 11, Jesus goes on to say about John:

"This is he of whom it is written,

'Behold, I send my messenger before your face,
who will prepare your way before you.'

Truly, I say to you, among those born of women there has arisen no one greater than John the Baptist. Yet the one who is least in the kingdom of heaven is greater than he."

John understood well the power of a surrendered life and the importance of waiting for the promise to be fulfilled. His life is an example that God keeps His promises, even when they take longer than we would like.

IT GETS BETTER

I believe that we should all have a life Scripture verse or motto that carries us through difficult seasons and reminds us why we should continue to press on in the face of difficulty. What is yours? Who is someone you know who has one?

When I think of John the Baptist, I think of Matthew 3:2, "Repent, for the kingdom of heaven is at hand." His life and death encompassed these words. They were at the core of who he was and what he believed. They reminded him of why he existed and what was worth dying for.

I have several. Some are personal, and others more practical.

I summarize my life verses with a single statement essential to my mission: Obedience to God is nonnegotiable.

That statement alone is central to the life I live for Christ and the choices I make.

It doesn't say obedience to God is easy, exciting, or optional. Although there are definitely times it can be easy and exciting, it should never be optional.

As important as our life Scripture or statement is, we also need words to carry us in seasons of transition. I like to call these Statements to Stand On. What Scriptures, words of truth, or statements do you grab hold of during seasons of change, challenge, and transition?

When doubt, worry, fear, and discouragement try to find a place on the throne of your heart, what do you say to remind yourself that glory comes in the waiting?

John the Baptist had a solid ground to stand on. He had a message and a mission that was far greater than he could imagine. That is why Jesus spoke these words in Matthew 11:11, "Truly, I say to you, among those born of women there has arisen no one greater than John the Baptist."

I want you to pay close attention here. Jesus said *has* arisen. Meaning before John, no one greater had come. Not Moses, Noah, Samuel, David, no one. However, after John, there would be one, *Jesus*. And still, before Jesus died, He spoke these words, "Truly,

truly, I say to you, whoever believes in me will also do the works that I do; and greater works than these will he do, because I am going to the Father" (John 14:12).

The ability to do great works went from John the Baptist to Jesus and now belongs to you and me. There is work to be done for the kingdom of God, and it will get done when obedience to God becomes a nonnegotiable.

LORD, PLEASE, SEND SOMEONE ELSE!

When I was a young girl, I would sit on the living room floor in front of the big, brown-box television completely mesmerized by the 1956 film *The Ten Commandments*. My dad, sitting in his chair, would alternate between reading his Bible and glancing at the screen as sounds of biblical history filled the room. During the movie, I often found myself imagining how different my life would be had I lived in the Bible days. No matter how many times I watched it, there was one particular scene that always captivated me and snatched me from daydreaming into reality.

The scene begins when Moses is holding the Ten Commandments on top of the mountain. In it, his face glowed with radiance from his mountain-top encounter with God, which was perfectly depicted through the TV screen. At that moment, Moses seemed like one of the bravest, most courageous, obedient servants of God.

And he was. However, to my surprise, as I started to study the Word, I quickly learned that this servant of God didn't start this way.

Moses—the one who God used to threaten Pharaoh, lead the Israelites out of Egypt, part the Red Sea, and deliver the Ten Commandments—spent a chapter and a half in the book of Exodus trying to convince God that he was not the man for the job. With excuse after excuse, Moses made every effort to get out of

God's request to help set His people free.

When I read the story of Moses, I am fascinated by how easily his list of excuses can be translated into some of my very own:

1. **Who am I to do this?** (Ex. 3:11) i.e., I can't do this, God; why did You pick me?
2. **Who are You that they should listen to me about You?** (Ex. 3:13) i.e., I am going to look like a fool in front of all these people.
3. **What if they don't believe You sent me?** (Ex. 4:1) i.e., These people aren't Christians; they won't understand or care.
4. **I'm not qualified.** (Ex. 4:10) i.e., I have no clue how to do this, and I can't learn right now!
5. **I don't want to do it.** (Ex. 4:13) i.e., I'm afraid; why are You asking *me* to do this?

This is really Moses' moment of truth in Exodus 4:13: "Oh, my Lord, please send someone else."

Lord, please, send someone else!

Many of us feel that way right now.

We feel ill-equipped or unqualified. Or, like Moses, we believe it will require us to return to people and places that we dread. We have legitimate fears and concerns that plague us each time we are reminded of the leap that God has told us to take.

> **God knows we won't have the capacity to carry the calling without facing the mountain.**

But just like Moses couldn't become "Moses, the Man on the Mountain" without first overcoming "Moses, the Man Running from the Mountain," God knows we won't have the capacity to carry the calling without facing the mountain.

When Moses had exhausted his list of excuses, God eventually became frustrated and allowed someone else to *help* him, but He didn't remove the responsibility from him. The same is true for us. God isn't going to take that responsibility away from you either. Just because we choose to delay doesn't mean He is going to choose someone else to do what we have been putting off. Although we may believe this, Moses, Jonah, and Jeremiah prove that avoidance does not remove our responsibility to complete the assignment.

Can I be honest here? Our human nature is to want things to be comfortable, simple, and easy. But comfortable, simple, and easy won't produce the Christlike character needed for the assignment God has created us to fulfill. Nothing Jesus did was comfortable, simple, or easy. But it was necessary. Obedience to God was a non-negotiable for Him, and it should be for us as well.

We must realize that we have been chosen to be His vessel that brings heaven to earth. The sooner we start our mission, the sooner He can get the glory out of His story in our lives.

When we understand the honor of being chosen by the Creator of the heavens and earth to bring forth His work upon the earth, our response becomes that of Samuel: "Speak, for your servant hears" (1 Sam. 3:10).

Or Mary, the mother of Jesus: "Behold, I am the servant of the Lord; let it be to me according to your word" (Luke 1:38).

CHAPTER 5

Favor Above Fear

I watched outside the room as my five-year-old son stood near the hallway that led into the family room. The hallway and family room were both dark; however, up the stairs shone a bright kitchen light where my husband stood waiting for him. My son, Aaron, has always been an extreme daddy's boy. This particular day, he was ready to head upstairs to my husband but there was a big problem. To get to the kitchen, he first had to overcome his fear of going through the dark rooms so he could climb the steps that led there.

I remember the look on his face when he realized the situation he was facing.

On the one hand, what he wanted was not far. But on the other hand, what he feared was way too close.

Everything in me wanted to save the day, to turn the lights on and to give him some reprieve. But I also knew we had been battling his intense fear of the dark for a while, and the better option would be to reassure him that he was covered on both sides so nothing harmful was going to happen to him.

As I prepared him for his adventure up the stairs with words of encouragement, I reminded him of 2 Timothy 1:7, which I always said to him when I knew he was afraid: "Remember, Aaron, God has not given you a spirit of fear but of power, love, and a sound mind."

He looked at me and repeated it as he always did, but this time he said something that took me by surprise: "I know, Mommy, but I'm still afraid."

At a loss for words, I somehow managed to reassure him that he would still be okay. He looked a few more times through the darkness and suddenly took off running like a lightning bolt through the hallway, past the family room, and up the stairs, just in time to grab his daddy as we cheered for his courageous decision.

BUT I'M STILL AFRAID

I pondered the words my son said for a while. There was such innocence and sincerity in his voice. It was as if he was saying, *Mommy, I know I don't have to be afraid, but I am. So, what now?*

As a parent, I understood that the fear he felt was paralyzing him and keeping him from something he wanted and would even be good for him. Removing the darkness may have made him more comfortable, but it wouldn't have helped him overcome his fear. Fear isn't something we want to find comfort in; it's something we want to fight against. Because fear doesn't just take a back seat, it has to be kicked out of the car completely or it will take over. It's not always easy to overcome it, but we don't have to do it alone.

You may be experiencing a type of fear right now as you're processing your leap. As a human, it's easy for us to justify our reason for fear, often leading us to settle for a lesser version of God's plan in a particular situation. When we operate in fear, the war within us puts our flesh's desire for comfort and ease against our spirit's longing for complete obedience to God. Fear is the enemy; faith is the ally. A war means someone has to be the winner, and we are on the winning side when we are in Christ.

Much like with my son, as we approach situations in our leap that require courage, the hidden fears that may have been preventing us from moving forward will rear their ugly head. Things such as:

Fear of financial loss
Fear of rejection
Fear of the unknown
Fear of failure
Fear of making a mistake
Fear of mishearing God

Name your fear(s) if I missed it. Those fears often develop before, or even as, we take on what God is calling us to do.

However, consider this: while my son was in the room *with* me, he felt comfortable and safe, but not satisfied. He wanted to be with my husband, and fear never likes when we want something it can't offer. Fear and courage don't work together; we have to put one down to pick up the other. Fear crept in the moment *where* my son stood didn't serve him anymore and he wanted something greater—something that couldn't be seen in the darkness but had been promised in the light.

So, what sat in the space between where he was and where he wanted to go? Honestly, the question isn't what was there, the real question is what he *believed* was there.

WHAT'S BEHIND THE FEAR

I'm not a fan of scary movies. I don't do scary things or places; it's just not my thing. However, I've seen enough of them in my youth to know that when you combine a dark, quiet room with a curious character, the odds are often not in their favor. The unknowns of what could or will happen next often create the suspense that sells to millions of viewers. But, when that same suspense is translated into our real world, it creates millions of people who stay locked up in the room of their fearful thoughts, afraid to find out what's on the other side of the door, in the dark valley, or standing between them and their future.

What we tend to forget in the face of fear is no matter what may be on the path or behind that door, God is with us. That is a promise made in Romans 8:28. But before we talk about that promise, let's first understand how fear gains ground and grows in our lives.

As an entrepreneur, one of the first things I learned was the difference between a goal and an objective. Loosely defined, a goal is the desired outcome in a situation, and the objectives are the small steps we will need to take to achieve the desired outcome.

Now, you may already be aware of this, but I want to remind you that the enemy of our soul has three main goals: to kill, steal, and destroy (John 10:10). And he works tirelessly day and night to achieve these goals. One of his greatest tools in this pursuit is fear. He uses it to kill our purpose, steal our future, and destroy our dedication. Take a moment and think back on how often you've seen him implement this tool in your life.

However, there are three primary ways, or objectives, he uses to plant the seed of fear in our lives: speculation, imagination, and negative thoughts.

Let's explore those words a little deeper.

The root word of *speculation* means "to take to be true on the basis of insufficient evidence."[1]

Imagination is defined as "the act or power of forming a mental image of something not present to the senses or never before wholly perceived in reality."[2]

Thoughts are defined as "something (such as an opinion or belief) in the mind."[3]

So, the enemy creates fear that paralyzes us through theories that lack evidence, mental images that are not part of our present or proven reality, and negative opinions and beliefs that don't line up with the truth of God.

Fear begins in our minds and plays out in our lives when we allow it. This is why we must be aware of what we are thinking so we're able to recognize who is planting the thought.

Similarly, one day while processing in my quiet time with God, I had a deep revelation on the topic of triggers. I'd been dealing with some triggers myself and wanted to understand the root cause of them. During this time, I realized that triggers began in my mind as a result of something said, sensed, or seen, but they are ultimately a counterfeit of discernment.

While a trigger can cause us to relive a negative past experience as if it's presently happening, discernment allows us to look at the current situation and leads us into truth about the matter. Discernment is an invitation to see the situation as God intended and not as our emotions intend. Fear can work as a trigger, telling a story that may not be true.

I invite you to consider, What story is fear telling you about leaping?

What negative thoughts have you had about it?

What have you imagined could happen?

What are you speculating?

Who do you believe is the author of those thoughts?

The truth is, no matter what comes our way as we journey in obedience to God's will, we have to remember that *God plans and Satan plots.* God is planning a good future for us; Satan is plotting a dead end. That dead end is not what God wants and neither do you.

Psalm 23 is so powerful. Allow me to remind you of these words written by David:

The LORD is my shepherd; I shall not want.
　　He makes me lie down in green pastures.
He leads me beside still waters.
　　He restores my soul.
He leads me in paths of righteousness
　　for his name's sake.

Even though I walk through the valley of the shadow
　　of death,
　　I will fear no evil,
for you are with me;
　　your rod and your staff,
　　they comfort me.

You prepare a table before me
　　in the presence of my enemies;
you anoint my head with oil;
　　my cup overflows.
Surely goodness and mercy shall follow me
　　all the days of my life,
and I shall dwell in the house of the LORD
　　forever.

This does not sound like a God whose plans are to lead us into a valley to destroy us. This psalm says, "He leads me in paths of righteousness." Now I've been on some less-than-righteous paths, but when I look back, I realize that I was doing the leading, not God. And even the more difficult paths that He has led me down, when I look back, I can completely see how He was glorified through that difficulty. It was a righteous path because He was right there with me. He was leading me down it so that He could reveal and release something to me that couldn't happen along an easier path, for reasons that I may not understand but I must trust.

And then this psalm says that when I am in the valley, He comforts me, prepares a table for me, and anoints me. We will talk more about this preparation in a later chapter, but I want you to pay close attention here. It seems to me like the unknown path I am most afraid of may lead me into the valley through which I will be most transformed.

And this is the moment where fear has to go from being a feeling to a foe. We must always remember: fear is a foe, not a friend.

SURRENDERING THE FEAR

Throughout the Bible, we see many of God's people exchange their greatest fears for God's great reward.

Do you remember the story of Joshua and the wall of Jericho in Joshua 6? In short, Joshua (preceded by Moses) and the men of war courageously march around the city of Jericho for seven days, and after the seventh time on the seventh day, the priests blow their horns and all the people shout as God instructed. Immediately, the walls of Jericho fall, allowing Joshua and the people of Israel to begin to take possession of the land that God promised them for over forty years. What a glorious story. But before all that took place, after Moses' death, God begins to speak to Joshua. Take a look at Joshua 1:1–9 with me:

> After the death of Moses the servant of the LORD, the LORD said to Joshua the son of Nun, Moses' assistant, "Moses my servant is dead. Now therefore arise, go over this Jordan, you and all this people, into the land that I am giving to them, to the people of Israel. Every place that the sole of your foot will tread upon I have given to you, just as I promised to Moses. From the wilderness and this Lebanon as far as the great river, the river Euphrates, all the land of the Hittites to the Great Sea toward the going down of the sun shall be your territory. No man shall be able to stand before you all the days of your life. Just as I was with Moses, so I will be with you. I will not leave you or forsake you. Be strong and courageous, for you shall cause this people to inherit the land that I swore to their fathers to give them. Only be strong and very courageous, being careful to do according to all the law that Moses my servant commanded you. Do not turn from it to the right hand or to the left, that you may have good success wherever you go. This Book of the Law shall not depart from your mouth, but you shall meditate on it day and night, so that you may be careful to do according to all that is written in it. For then you will make your way prosperous, and then you will have good success. Have I not commanded you? Be strong and courageous. Do not be frightened, and do not be dismayed, for the LORD your God is with you wherever you go.

Here is what I want you to see from this passage. Joshua was given a new assignment as the leader of the people of Israel. In this new role, he was promised both God's presence and favor (vv. 3–5).

However, he was also warned to do two very significant things: steward the favor well and surrender the fear (vv. 7–9). These are the same expectations God has for us. He wants us to know that we have access to His presence and favor, but we must be ready to steward the favor and surrender the fear.

TELL FEAR WHO'S BOSS

When my youngest daughter was a toddler, like most, she didn't like being told what to do by her older siblings. At the time, she was the youngest of five older siblings. There were times when she would listen, and other times, she would simply remind them that although she was small, so were they, and she had no obligation to obey them. Her favorite line was, "You're not the boss of me. Daddy and Mommy are!" Of course, we would correct her and remind her that as long as they were telling her the right thing to do, she needed to listen since they were older. She didn't like that too much but would oblige.

When I think about this thing called fear, I want us to have the same attitude my daughter had, because when we become children of God, fear isn't in charge—God is. God will never tell us, "Well, fear is kind of in charge if it's telling you the right things to do." Fear that drives us in the opposite direction of where God is leading is of the enemy. Fear wasn't created to tell us what is right; it was created to deceive us and strip us of our power.

Remember what the angel said to Mary in Luke 1:30–31: "And the angel said to her, 'Do not be afraid, Mary, for you have found favor with God. And behold, you will conceive in your womb and bear a son, and you shall call his name Jesus.'"

Jesus' introduction into the world came by way of a fear-for-favor exchange. When the angel Gabriel came to inform Mary of what was to come and that she had found favor with God, he first instructed her to release her fear. Fear can impede our ability to clearly hear what God is telling us. Perhaps Mary first had to release her fear in order to come into the knowledge of the favor she had.

Joshua had to obey in the face of fear so he could gain the wisdom needed to lead well with God, and we must do the same. When we surrender our fear, we are not abandoning the awareness of danger that may be present; we may even still *feel* afraid. But we are inviting God into that space and trusting that His wisdom and discernment will occupy and lead us in how to respond to any situation.

FAREWELL TO FEAR

We have spent this entire chapter discussing the root and role of fear and many of you may be thinking, So now what? How do I get rid of the fear I am feeling about taking this leap? Will it just go away? It certainly can, but let's set ourselves up with a better strategy.

The Bible tells us in James 4:7, "Submit yourselves therefore to God. Resist the devil, and he will flee from you." This Scripture applies to many areas, including fear, as we walk with Christ. When fear begins to speak to us through imagination, speculation, or negative thoughts, we must resist it. Through an intentional act of surrender and obedience, we submit our will to God and replace the lies of the enemy with the truth God has spoken.

Nelson Mandela once said, "The brave man is not he who does not feel afraid, but he who conquers that fear."[4] But Solomon said it best when he said, "The fear of the LORD is the beginning of wisdom, and the knowledge of the Holy One is insight" (Prov. 9:10). This is the only fear we should have; every other kind should be conquered with Christ.

I understand that some things are easier said than done, so I want to end this chapter by sharing some helpful ways to move beyond fear so you can start experiencing God's abundant plan for your life:

1. Identify and pray about the things you're most afraid of.
2. Find Scripture to speak and declare when you begin to feel fear trying to occupy space in your life.
3. Read stories of courageous leaders in the Bible.
4. Read Christian authors who help you find courage through their stories and words.
5. Allow worship to wash over your fearful heart through psalms and songs.

Remember, abundant life is found beyond the limits of fear. It's time to live abundantly.

Leapers Make History

CHAPTER 6

The Fisherman's Leap

Starting a podcast was never on my radar. It took multiple suggestions from my husband, and the surprising confirmation of a friend, for me to yield to God's leading in this. I just couldn't see the need or how I had the time. Both became very clear once I started, and I can admit that hosting a podcast has been one of my greatest rewards. I've had the honor of meeting some of the most amazing people and hearing their stories in my role as a host (God knew the blessing this podcast would be, which is why I'm so thankful He didn't give in to my whining).

A few of those stories stand out to me. One is from guest Kevin Anselmo, author of *Reframing Career Success*.

Kevin grew up learning some entrepreneurial skills from his father, who was a plumber. Although he jokes about not being gifted with any plumbing talent, Kevin recognized that when he became an adult, he knew he eventually wanted the freedom and experience of entrepreneurship. As time passed, Kevin graduated from college and took a job across the world in Europe. During our time together, he shared how he'd become accustomed to the culture and people, and often enjoyed being the only American in the offices where he worked. He also met his wife during his ten-year stay there. His experience and memories were great, but opportunity called, leading him back to the States.

After a decade in Europe, Kevin was offered a job at Duke University. His return was a more difficult leap for him than his original move to Europe. He said it was because in the original move, he was much younger and had fewer family responsibilities, and more freedom. This perspective resonated with me as I've learned that it's easier for us to take leaps when we're younger than it is when we become adults and are more established.

Kevin worked at Duke for approximately two years but saw it as an opportunity for him to formulate a personal business venture. I'm always amazed when someone gets to work for an organization that others could only dream about but decides to leave for a bigger dream. People like Kevin learn to see every opportunity as a potential steppingstone toward living out their calling, and not as a stopping point. This has happened so many times in my life too. I've come to realize that when we surrender our dreams to God, we're not limited by what others might be satisfied with. We see every opportunity as an opportunity to obey God and to do His will.

Throughout Kevin's story, his longing for entrepreneurship didn't wane as he planned his career moves with his end goal in mind—to own his own company.

During his two years at the university, he'd work full-time while calculating for the financial needs of his family when he went into full-time entrepreneurship. After some time of prayer and planning, he realized that he needed at least one client as an anchor to cover at least sixty percent of his Duke salary. That was his sustainability number.

When that one client appeared in his inbox, he was ready to take the full leap. He left his job at the university and started his company, Experiential Communications. Over the past decade, he has worked with multiple clients along the way. Amazingly, his salary has never dropped lower than the sustainability number, and he has certainly experienced God's great abundance.[1]

Kevin, like many of us, had to step outside his comfort zone to experience the greater life God had in store for him. Although he always had a desire to become an entrepreneur, it wasn't until he chose to turn that *nudge* into *now* that he was able to walk out the rest of the perfect path God had laid out for him.

A MEANS TO AN END

What does it take to follow Jesus?

Well, for Peter (remember, we will focus on his journey as a disciple for this leap), it took walking away from all he knew and owned, and intentionally embracing His divine plan for his life.

The moment Peter met Jesus and was called out of his job as a fisherman and into his role as a disciple was unexpected but predestined by God. Being a fisherman may have been a dream job or simply a means to an end, similar to Kevin's career at Duke. Either way, it was the path God used to lead Peter toward his eternal purpose.

Allow me to give you a little context about Peter's journey to becoming one of the fishers of men. Matthew 4:18–22 says,

> While walking by the Sea of Galilee, he saw two brothers, Simon (who is called Peter) and Andrew his brother, casting a

net into the sea, for they were fishermen. And he said to them, "Follow me, and I will make you fishers of men." Immediately they left their nets and followed him. And going on from there he saw two other brothers, James the son of Zebedee and John his brother, in the boat with Zebedee their father, mending their nets, and he called them. Immediately they left the boat and their father and followed him.

Peter, as well as the other men, were fishermen by trade. There are different debates about whether this was a lucrative career or if it was one that barely supplied their basic needs, but one thing that can't be debated is that it was a job. They had to be skilled and trained in how to be a good fisherman, and often that training started when they were quite young.

God can always do more with our willingness than He could ever do with our worthiness.

Here is what I'd like to think: when Jesus went to look for someone who had the potential to be a good fisher of men, He first examined who had proven potential in being skilled at catching fish. The person had to be someone skilled at what he was already putting his hands to or someone willing to get better. Meaning, he may not have always caught lots of fish, but he was willing to try.

God can always do more with our willingness than He could ever do with our worthiness. I dare to believe that if the skill wasn't there, the willingness and fortitude were, and that's what God had been cultivating in Peter and the others to prepare them for the work He was calling them into. These "fishermen" were born to "fish for men," and it took their walking away from the familiar and choosing to follow Jesus so they could experience the life He had in store.

FROM FISH TO MEN

As with any leap, there is an initial preparation that occurs. For Peter, it was being skilled in fishing or at least being a fisherman. Through this vocation, he learned to be patient, persistent, and undaunted. These same skills helped Peter to serve Jesus well during His time of public ministry here on earth. The key word is that Peter served Jesus *well*, not perfectly. These same traits are found in many modern-day fishermen leapers and are required to take the Fisherman's Leap.

When it comes to the Fisherman's Leap, the person, much like with a fisherman disciple, has been called to leave their career and go fully into something God has instructed them to do. It could be starting a business, ministry, nonprofit, etc. Whatever it may be, it will require a drastic shift from "what currently is" to "what will be."

There's so much beauty and wonder that comes from this leap, but it can come with a huge burden in the area of provision if we don't recognize how God is leading us to use our current season to prepare for our leap. It can be both exciting and intimidating as the hope for a well-thought-out plan works out as planned. The feeling of overwhelm can easily claim a seat in your life as you leave everything you know and step into a world of unknowns.

I want you to pause and consider how exciting this moment is: to be handpicked by God to fulfill His work on earth through the Fisherman's Leap, a work that is not only going to bless you, but many others whose lives will be transformed by your single act of obedience and courage. Because the call to make a leap isn't just about what we will *do* but who we will *serve*. If you allow it, this will draw you closer to Him and deeper in your walk with Christ. You're about to experience God's miraculous nature in your life like never before through this leap. It's going to feel like walking on water!

PREPARE TO "WALK ON WATER"

Peter had done many things in and on the water as a fisherman. He swam, caught fish, mended nets, and slept in boats, but I'd suspect he never imagined he could walk on water.

In Matthew 14:28–33, we are met with a moment when the consistent nature of God meets an inconsistent belief of His creation.

And Peter answered him, "Lord, if it is you, command me to come to you on the water." He said, "Come." So Peter got out of the boat and walked on the water and came to Jesus. But when he saw the wind, he was afraid, and beginning to sink he cried out, "Lord, save me." Jesus immediately reached out his hand and took hold of him, saying to him, "O you of little faith, why did you doubt?" And when they got into the boat, the wind ceased. And those in the boat worshiped him, saying, "Truly you are the Son of God."

Now, if you're like me, this passage of Scripture is very familiar. I remember hearing this story often in Sunday school, and admittedly, it's become a bit common in my archive of biblical texts. However, since the Bible is a living Word, we should always ask God to reveal deeper revelation about a text so it can be fresh and relevant in our lives. Allow me to share a unique perspective.

Peter walking on water is extraordinary, yet quite consistent with the nature of God as a Creator. Romans 1:20 tells us, "For his invisible attributes, namely, his eternal power and divine nature, have been clearly perceived, ever since the creation of the world, in the things that have been made. So, they are without excuse."

Consider with me for a moment: Doesn't it seem probable, if not possible, that the same God whose nature is revealed through the peculiar and majestic things that we see upon the earth would have the ability to empower a person to walk *on* water? He reveals His power and glory every day. The wonders of the world speak of the glory of His hand. The things we see as ordinary are truly *extraordinary* when we acknowledge His power in it. The awe and wonder of the work of the Lord come as a result of fighting against the familiarity that breeds contempt. We have to fight against the temptation to perceive His glory as less glorious or His daily miracles as less miraculous. Everything we see functioning in extraordinary ways speaks of His nature as a powerful and purposeful Creator.

Before Peter walked on water, Jesus did. He didn't call Peter to do anything He hadn't already done or conquer anything He hadn't already conquered, including overcoming fear. If you pay close attention to God's nature, you will notice how God always does things first. Before there were children, God created humans. Before there were ships, God directed Noah to build an ark. Before there were churches, God led Bezalel to help construct the tabernacle. The list could go on and on.

We see this same pattern as we read Matthew 14:23–27:

> And after he had dismissed the crowds, he went up on the
> mountain by himself to pray. When evening came, he was
> there alone, but the boat by this time was a long way from
> the land, beaten by the waves, for the wind was against
> them. And in the fourth watch of the night he came to them,
> walking on the sea. But when the disciples saw him walking
> on the sea, they were terrified, and said, "It is a ghost!" and they
> cried out in fear. But immediately Jesus spoke to them, saying,
> "Take heart; it is I. Do not be afraid."

I want you to recognize that Jesus' pattern is to go with and before us, so He is fully aware of the leap ahead of us.

As mentioned before about the early skills of Peter's fishing career, what he needed to survive was found in the water. However, as a fisher of men, what he needed to sustain him was found outside of the water: Jesus.

The story of Peter and the disciples is a reminder for us as we take the Fisherman's Leap. It reveals that our fear of what's beyond the water shouldn't hinder us from trusting in the God who leads us to walk on the water. I love what Jesus does with Peter in Matthew 14:31 when he was beginning to sink beneath the waves. The Bible says, "Jesus immediately *reached out his hand and took hold of him.*"

Peter's sinking wasn't an indication of failing; it's an indication of fearing.

What a beautiful moment. Jesus didn't ignore Peter sinking or tell him to pull himself up. Jesus acknowledged the need and reached out His hand to help His disciple and friend. He didn't want Peter to sink, and He doesn't want you to either.

Peter's sinking wasn't an indication of failing; it's an indication of fearing. Since we now know that fear is a foe, when the weight of fear is causing us to sink, we can look for God's hand to lift us up. We're not leaping alone.

CHAPTER 7

The Shepherd's Leap

After having our youngest son, my husband and I moved into the home of our dreams in the city I consider my worst nightmare. It wasn't a terrible city by any means—just not the place I wanted to settle.

We'd both written out what we wanted in a dream home, and our initial search started with minimally communicating our lists to one another. We spent months looking at houses online and going with our realtor for viewings, yet never found the one we felt we could call home. To top it off, we were expecting our youngest son at the time, so the patience factor wasn't at its peak for me. If only someone would have warned us that pregnancy and home buying weren't good companions!

One day, at the height of our home search, my husband suggested that we pause and pray over our home request. It was then that we realized we were aiming toward two different targets. He wanted a fixer upper, and I wanted a walk-in ready home. He wanted lots of land, and I wanted very little land. He was open to living just about anywhere, and I was very specific about where I wanted to live. I shared my hesitation in moving to the east side of the city, and he shared his resolve. We both wanted what was best concerning our move but saw things from different perspectives. We both considered what the family needed but in different ways.

I can honestly say that after our prayer and talk, something shifted.

We reached out to the realtor (who happened to be a friend) and told her we were open to looking on the near east side of the city since we had not found what we were looking for yet. She sent us several listings, and within a day or two, we were viewing homes on that side of town.

One thing I must have failed to tell my realtor friend was that there was one specific city I still had on my "no" list. As it turns out, it must have been God leading me down His path and not my own.

As we wrapped up our viewings one day, we were left with one home in one city to visit. I was exhausted, and on this particular day, we had our children with us who were now ready to end this field trip, eat dinner, and have real fun.

As we headed back to the car, I told my realtor friend not to worry about taking us to the last house; I knew I wouldn't want to live there anyway. That house happened to be on the "no" list I mentioned earlier. However, since we were only about five minutes away from that house, my husband convinced me that it didn't make sense not to take a look. Begrudgingly, I agreed, and we headed to the property.

My husband entered first, and I heard all his oohs and aahs as he traveled through the house. I had to admit that upon entering this home, something felt different. I started to walk around the house and realized it had every single thing we'd come to agree upon, written down, and prayed for—and more. The home was beautiful. I didn't know whether I was happy that we found the right home or disappointed that it was located in the "wrong" city!

Well, that home became our home. It was the house I loved in the city I would come to love.

It's funny when I think about how adamant I'd been concerning where I *didn't* want to live. I had no understanding, at the time, that every move should be orchestrated and ordained by God. When we move from city to city, state to state, or country to country, we should be fulfilling an assignment. Although I spent months going around the proverbial "mountain," looking at homes in a completely different place, God knew exactly where I was going to end up. He was just patiently waiting for me to agree with what He'd already ordained.

My list of reasons not to move to this city was long. They were all rational and legitimate concerns: higher taxes, questionable school system, and few families with children. However, now my list of reasons not to move *from* it is even longer. I love the teachers and the diversity of the community. We have the best neighbor in the world who has taken my children in as his surrogate grandchildren. The size of the home is perfect for our large, growing family. I've had the opportunity to respond to the prayer assignment for this city more than any other previous city I've lived in, and I've seen prayers answered for this town that have been waiting for decades.

As I consider the lessons I learned during that season, I've concluded that when God calls us to relocate, it isn't always about personal aspirations or agendas. It's all about divine assignments and blessing, often impacting generations to come. Similarly, this lesson is what Abram learned on his journey to Canaan.

Then I ponder the words of Elisabeth Elliot, who explains the beautiful working together of our will and God's will:

We have said that Christian discipline is one's wholehearted yes to the call of God. It is of the highest importance that we understand the necessity of two wills, the one created by the other and ordained free, both operating in accord. If we forget that there are two and dwell only on the sovereign will of God, we will abdicate our responsibility and lapse into the fatalism of Islam, which leaves all to the inscrutable and unknowable. If, on the other hand, we forget the sovereignty of God and see ourselves as independent, we will arrogate to ourselves all responsibility and leave God out of it—in other words, we make ourselves God. In both cases we fail to do His will, and the result is the forfeiting of our joy and freedom.[1]

She says that "God has arranged things in such a way that His own action is coupled with the action of men."[2] And this is how and when we experience the Shepherd's Leap on full display.

UNFINISHED BUSINESS

One thing I've loved about being an adult Christian is going back to biblical stories I heard in Sunday school and reading the full, unedited, adult version of the story. It's mind-blowing in many ways to see how much wasn't shared to help preserve my innocence. For example, when we hear the story of Jonah in Sunday school and learn about his resistance to delivering God's warning to Nineveh, we think the story about that city ends with him giving them the message and the people changing their ways. They do, and the city is spared, but the story doesn't end there. In the book of Nahum, the prophet predicts the eventual destruction of Nineveh because of the people's "unceasing evil" (3:19). Another example is how different the movie version of Moses' calling is compared to the story in Scripture that shows us how adamant Moses was about convincing God he didn't want to deliver God's people out of Egypt. But the story of Abram shocked me the most! For years I'd been led to believe that when Abram left Haran under the instructions of the Lord, he had no clue where he was going. The misconception is that God told him to go, and Abram just started aimlessly walking.

As I mentioned before, here's what I found as I started to study the Scriptures: Abram was not blindly or pennilessly leaving his country. He knew exactly where he was heading and had the financial provision to go there. So why did God tell him, "Go from your country and kindred and your father's house to the land that I will show you" (Gen. 12:1)?

In chapter 2, we saw that this is the Scripture most people use when they want to take a leap of faith but are unsure about where they are going next or how they are to do it without financial provision. It's been interpreted and misinterpreted often, and my hope is that you will walk away with a proper understanding of this moment between God and Abram and how it applies to your own life.

First, Abram was a shepherd. In our minds, we might associate being a shepherd with a less-than-prestigious career path. However, Abram was known to be one of the wealthiest people in the Bible. If we pause and read Genesis 13:2, it says, "Now Abram was very rich in livestock, in silver, and in gold." We also read, "And Abram took Sarai his wife, and Lot his brother's son, and all their possessions that they had gathered" (Gen. 12:5).

Despite how he obtained his wealth, the fact is when Abram left Haran, he had much to work with and little to worry about, financially.

We also discussed previously that Abram knew where he was headed. Take another look at Genesis 11:31, "Terah took Abram his son and Lot the son of Haran, his grandson, and Sarai his daughter-in-law, his son Abram's wife, and they went forth together from Ur of the Chaldeans to go into the land of Canaan, *but when they came to Haran, they settled there.*" This Scripture is significant because it reveals that Abram's father, Terah, was headed to Canaan but made a pit stop in Haran. It never said he was headed to Haran; it said that he settled there, even until his death. Starting again in Genesis 12:1–7, let's bring it all together:

> Now the LORD said to Abram, "Go from your country and your kindred and your father's house to the land that I will show you. And I will make of you a great nation, and I will bless you and make your name great, so that you will be a blessing. I will bless those who bless you, and him who dishonors you I will curse, and in you all the families of the earth shall be blessed."
>
> So Abram went, as the LORD had told him, and Lot went with him. Abram was seventy-five years old when he departed from Haran. And Abram took Sarai his wife, and Lot his brother's son, and all their possessions that they had gathered, and the people that they had acquired in Haran, *and they set out to go to the land of Canaan.* When they came to the land of Canaan, Abram passed through the land to the place at Shechem, to the oak of Moreh. At that time the Canaanites were in the land. Then the LORD appeared to Abram and said,

"To your offspring I will give this land." So he built there an altar to the LORD, who had appeared to him.

When we consider that Terah, Abram's father, stopped short of his intent to reach Canaan but Abram, upon his father's death, set out for Canaan with his abundance, the misinterpreted storyline completely changes. What God spoke in Genesis 12:1 was intended to separate and sanctify Abram, but also to shepherd him into his place of promise.

When reconsidering this progression, we first realize that Abram's journey was not starting; it was actually continuing. I believe Abram's assignment was to complete the journey his father Terah had begun—to head to Canaan—so God could release His unchanging plan to him. *The Moody Bible Commentary* explains that Terah was a pagan worshiper but took the lead in setting out for Canaan after Abram received the call by God "when he was in Mesopotamia, before he lived in Haran" (Acts 7:2).[3] Whether Terah was aware or not, he set the direction for his family and positioned them for the plans God had already established and would eventually share with Abram.

Second, we learn that Abram was traveling with financial provision and was very prepared for the journey ahead. In all this, we see that God patiently waited until Abram was ready to receive the promise spoken to him in Genesis 12:7, "To your offspring I will give this land."

When God told Abram to go to the land that He would show him, He was not telling him to leave everything behind and go to an unknown location. Instead, He was inviting him to travel intentionally down the path with the provision He had given him (see Gen. 13:2). Canaan may not have been where Abram was to settle, but it was certainly where he knew he was supposed to head. Abram wasn't a sheep without a shepherd walking aimlessly; he was being led by the Good Shepherd, intentionally, and so are we.

THE MAKING OF A SHEPHERD'S LEAP

If we assume for a moment that Terah was actually supposed to lead his family to Canaan, then it would be safe to say that he stopped short of fulfilling a very important and significant assignment. As a parent, I think of the potential delay he caused to the next generation because he settled. Similar to considering who you are "walking on water" for, also consider whose future will be impacted when you shift instead of settle.

> Similar to considering who you are "walking on water" for, also consider whose future will be impacted when you shift instead of settle.

I understand that it's easy to become comfortable at the halfway mark and choose to settle for known security and stability over uncertainty. What if Terah had followed the one true God? Would he have settled in Haran and died at a pit stop? I believe God never intended Terah to die at a pit stop, and He doesn't intend the same for us. However, if I can be honest, more than once in my life I have been more like Terah than Abram, turning a pit stop into a permanent stop.

Even as I was writing this book, I ran into a situation where I questioned if I was mimicking Terah, stopping short of completing the journey. But then I recalled two objectives that God provides with any leap, but especially a Shepherd's Leap: *a preordained path* and *predetermined provision.*

This is essential for the person making this leap to understand.

Much like with Abram, the person called to take the Shepherd's Leap is being commissioned to relocate so that they can occupy the new territory God is wanting them to have. It could be a new city, state, or country. It could be for a job, ministry, or unknown reason that will become clearer once you get there. Relocation could be from place to place or position to position. Although there are some factors that are known, such as where you're going and the provision to get there, what might make this leap seem difficult are the things that are unknown.

What are you supposed to do when you get there?
Where will you find community and support?
How long will you be there?

These questions might create stress or anxiety around the leap, leading you to stall or delay despite the known factors. When wisdom and worry are difficult to distinguish, this is an indicator that we don't have our ear tuned completely to God's heart. I want you to remember that although unknowns may be unavoidable, trust in God should be our guide.

Remember what the Bible tells us: "Do not be anxious about anything, but in everything by prayer and supplication with thanksgiving let your requests be made known to God" (Phil. 4:6).

Scripture also encourages us to "trust in the LORD with all your heart, and do not lean on your own understanding. In all your ways acknowledge him, and he will make straight your paths" (Prov. 3:5–6).

Just like God gave Abram a clear path and provision, He will do the same for you. He will be a lamp unto your feet, allowing you to see the next step, and a light unto your path (see Ps. 119:105), making the road ahead clear and bright.

However, there is something we should begin to understand as we position our hearts for the leaps ahead: the act of letting go.

LESSONS IN LETTING GO

I listed a few unknowns that we often consider when we are being led into new territory. As you read that list, what came to mind? How did you feel?

The truth is, letting go is not easy, no matter what circumstances may lead to that moment. There is an unwanted but absolutely warranted purging and pruning that happens as part of the Shepherd's Leap. The anticipation of that process is often what makes the leap feel unbearable. Relationships are lost, communities are left, and lifestyles are shifted. It's a difficult transition for everyone involved because the present is clear, but the future is blurry.

If you have children, this adds another layer to the leap. It impacts each one differently and tests both their resilience and risk-taking capacity. We can pray and prepare them as best we can, but we can't prevent them from going through the emotions of the transition. They, like us, are learning to let go and trust the process of new beginnings.

Brandi Morris, founder of Light to Live By, shared on episode 41 of my podcast about her Shepherd's Leap with her daughter. In the episode she talks about her move from Memphis to Washington, DC, to support her church's new plant. She not only authentically walks us through the way she prepared practically and spiritually, but also how she navigated the tough conversation with her daughter. In the episode, I gained three key takeaways:

1. When God places the seed in your heart, treasure it until He gives you the next step.
2. When He reveals the next step, take it, no matter how big

or small it may seem because it becomes both an act of obedience and agreement.

3. Pray for God to touch your child's heart before presenting them with the news of a move; however, once you present it, allow them to process through their emotions as you pray that God would reveal His heart to them.

But there was one more crossroads moment that changed everything for Brandi. In the interview she said:

I remember one day, just sitting at my desk in my house, feeling really overwhelmed. . . . And I just thought to myself, *What if I don't do it? What if I don't go?* And I thought, *What would that look like?* And as I thought about it, I said, "I cannot go [in]to the end of the year and this church campus opens, and I'm still here in Memphis. Because I will know that I missed it. And not because I innocently missed it . . . but because I willfully decided to disobey. I cannot let that be my story."[4]

Brandi allowed her overwhelm to lead her to obedience, and we can too. We will all be faced with a crossroads moment: a moment when we must choose between willful obedience or willful disobedience. What choice will you make?

CHAPTER 8

The Builder's Leap

I f ever there was a person I've seen care for someone well, it is my friend Lauren. Lauren and I have known each other since preschool. Although there were seasons when we would barely talk or see each other due to life transitions, when we would come back in contact, it was as if we never missed a beat.

Even still, I remember one day while still in high school having an issue with my first car and meeting Lauren's dad for the first time. He was kind, funny, caring, and clearly a great father. This was proven even more as he took out time to look over my car, even though this was my first time meeting him, as if I were also his daughter. Lauren and I are both daddy's girls, so I know an amazing dad when I see one!

After high school, Lauren went away to college in Florida but returned to Ohio to care for her dad, whose serious medical conditions caused him to need twenty-four-hour assistance in a nursing home. Shortly after she returned, she went to cosmetology school and started styling hair full-time, eventually becoming the stylist for my girls and me. Hair appointments were more than just the average time in the shop—these were also great reasons to spend an extra long time with a friend where we would talk, laugh, share stories, and encourage each other through difficult seasons.

Although Lauren was very good at her job, the hair industry wasn't helping meet her financial or personal goals. After several years as a stylist, she also took on a full-time position at an insurance company with great pay and benefits. The demand of two jobs, while still being a caregiver for her father, was stretching her thin. She was overwhelmed, overworked, and depleted. About two years into her new role, her level of stress had skyrocketed.

One day while doing my hair, she shared how her dad had called her in tears because the conditions at the nursing home had become so unbearable. Lauren knew that her home couldn't accommodate his medical needs, but she decided it'd be best to figure out how to bring him home with her. She spent several days looking for handicap accommodations, scheduling transportation services for his dialysis, and more. She knew she was taking on a huge responsibility, but watching him suffer in the nursing home was not an option.

After her father moved in with her, she decided to take time off under the Family Medical Leave Act so she could better handle his daily needs. The choice was stressful, hard, and very emotional. Sadly, shortly after moving in, her father passed one day while away for treatment.

I always tell Lauren that she was an amazing daughter; I don't know if she believes me yet, but it's true. I admired her sacrificial, advocating, and servant heart as a daughter and caregiver, even to the point of taking on the full responsibility of moving her father into her home when the nursing home facility wasn't properly caring for him.

Like anyone, she had moments when she felt completely in over her head, and she was. But her love for her father reminded her that it was worth the weight of the responsibility.

This is the truth that Nehemiah knew as he stepped out to take the Builder's Leap.

WORTH THE WEIGHT

Nehemiah understood the weight of shifting his life to care for people he loved.

When he was advanced in years, he was called to temporarily leave his position as cupbearer to King Artaxerxes and help the exiled Jews rebuild the wall of Jerusalem. The wall protected the people from being attacked by their enemies, and the strength of the wall was a sign of God's presence with His people.[1]

One day Nehemiah, who was part of the family of Jewish exiles held captive in Babylon, was met by his brother, Hanani. Hanani was compelled to meet his brother, Nehemiah, and speak with him about the terrible condition of the wall and the threat and disgrace to the people. After being destroyed centuries earlier, the wall had still not been rebuilt, and they needed his help. The news seemed to come as a shock and concern to Nehemiah. Immediately, the burden of this request, due to the "great trouble and shame" (Neh. 1:3) the people were experiencing, consumed him: "As soon as I heard these words I sat down and wept and mourned for days, and I continued fasting and praying before the God of heaven" (v. 4).

Nehemiah's first response to a request of this magnitude was prayer and fasting. Finishing out the rest of Nehemiah chapter 1, we see the burden of his heart. Several verses are prayers and petitions to God on behalf of the people and the proposition. Similar to Jesus, Nehemiah's heart was to see his people free, protected, and restored.

Scripture doesn't tell us about all the secret prayers Nehemiah spoke leading up to this petition in chapter 1. However, I would like to assume that he talked to God about things like his fear of approaching the king about the matter. *Who would take over his role? Where would the provision come from? How would the people respond to his leadership?*

I can only imagine the toiling he went through as he lay awake at night seeking the hand and the heart of God in this matter. He knew it was going to require a sacrifice that he had never seen anyone else do—namely, approaching the king's throne and asking for permission to fulfill this work.

The flesh desires comfort and career, and the soul desires security and assurance. But the spirit desires obedience to the will of God. It would be great if all three of them were always in sync, but more often, they are at war with each other. However, there is one authority that should control them all: God.

Nehemiah's choice to submit to God's will allowed him to process his emotions and sorrow while still honoring God in moving forward. That is my hope for you as you read through this chapter. Nehemiah's decision wasn't easy; it was a huge risk and sacrifice, but God was good and gave him exactly what he would need. However, he would first need to confront the conflict.

CONFRONTING THE CONFLICT

As Nehemiah worked through the possible issues *within* himself concerning this leap, as well as his deep sorrow over the "great trouble and disgrace" the people were experiencing (1:3 NLT), he became clearer on how to address the issues *around* him. He would have three major obstacles to defeat along the journey: approaching the king, the people, and his enemies. Let's see how he handled each of them, starting with the king.

> And the king said to me, "Why is your face sad, seeing you are not sick? This is nothing but sadness of the heart." Then I was very much afraid. I said to the king, "Let the king live forever! Why should not my face be sad, when the city, the place of my fathers' graves, lies in ruins, and its gates have been destroyed by fire?" Then the king said to me, "What are you requesting?" So I prayed to the God of heaven. And I said to the king, "If it pleases the king, and if your servant has found favor in your sight, that you send me to Judah, to the city of my fathers' graves, that I may rebuild it." And the king said to me (the queen sitting beside him), "How long will you be gone, and when will you return?" So it pleased the king to send me when I had given him a time. (Neh. 2:2–6)

That turned around beautifully! What was once an obstacle—approaching the king—had become an opportunity that would set him up for success in his assignment. Now let's move on to the next obstacle, the people.

> Now there arose a great outcry of the people and of their wives against their Jewish brothers. ". . . Now our flesh is as the flesh of our brothers, our children are as their children. Yet we are forcing our sons and our daughters to be slaves, and some of our daughters have already been enslaved, but it is not in our power to help it, for other men have our fields and our vineyards." (Neh. 5:1, 5)

During the rebuilding process, Nehemiah encountered opposition from the Jews who were working alongside him. One day, some Jews approached him during the rebuilding of the wall to make him aware of how they were being treated. Nehemiah learned that the wealthier Jews were enslaving the impoverished ones due to debts owed. Since they were mistreating their own people, the matter needed to be dealt with because it threatened the integrity and honor of the community. What good would it do to build a wall that stopped enemies from coming into the city if there was disunity and conflict among the people who occupied the city? They might eventually destroy themselves if no one else did. Nehemiah took on the task of settling it.

> "We, as far as we are able, have bought back our Jewish brothers who have been sold to the nations, but you even sell your brothers that they may be sold to us! . . . The thing that you are doing is not good. Ought you not to walk in the fear of our God to prevent the taunts of the nations our enemies? Moreover, I and my brothers and my servants are lending them money and grain. Let us abandon this exacting of interest. Return to them this very day their fields, their vineyards, their olive orchards, and their houses, and the percentage of money, grain, wine, and oil that you have been exacting from them." Then they said, "We will restore these and require nothing from them. We will do as you say." And I called the priests and made them swear to do as they had promised. (Neh. 5:8–12)

Now that the unity of the people had been restored, they could continue to rebuild the wall. Since they now saw each other as equals within society, they could focus on the assignment and overcoming the obstacles, together.

The final obstacle of the enemy was an ongoing issue for Nehemiah as he worked on rebuilding the wall. The greatest threat or obstacle originally presented itself in the storyline in chapter 4 in the form of oppressive opposition to the completion of his assignment led by a few groups and individuals.

But when Sanballat and Tobiah and the Arabs and the Ammonites and the Ashdodites heard that the repairing of the walls of Jerusalem was going forward and that the breaches were beginning to be closed, they were very angry. And they all plotted together to come and fight against Jerusalem and to cause confusion in it. And we prayed to our God and set a guard as a protection against them day and night. (vv. 7–9)

Nehemiah addressed each obstacle practically and spiritually with prayer and strategy. Despite the adversity he faced along the way, he was committed to finishing the work of rebuilding the wall, and he did it in just fifty-two days (see Neh. 6:15).

Here is what I want you to take note of: for Nehemiah, it wasn't a matter of avoiding the obstacles; it was a matter of overcoming them. Although he had many limitations—such as time, resources, and even opposition from his own people—he served a God who is limitless. Each part of the leap presented challenges he had to overcome in different ways, and I'm sure he became a bit discouraged. Ease would have been a more convenient companion in the process than difficulty. However, through overcoming these difficulties, he was able to experience unbelievable victory and success.

My question to you is if Nehemiah could persevere and withstand to accomplish great work in just fifty-two days, what great work can we accomplish in the fifty-two weeks in a year that we are given?

LED-BY-THE-BUILDER'S LEAP

The person called to the Builder's Leap is being led by God to complete a task or assignment within a specific season that requires a sacrifice of time, talent, or treasure. That task may be caring for a loved one, working on a short-term project such as a book, or getting a business or ministry off the ground. No matter how big or small, the assignment will require their undivided attention and sacrifice for a season, usually leading to a temporary or seemingly permanent relief of their current, full-time duties in some capacity.

Throughout this leap, there are several emotions we may find ourselves feeling that might charge and encourage us, or drain and discourage us. This is often due to the challenge of balancing necessity and need.

When we are presented with the need to help our loved one, it can become a burden. I'm not implying that *they* are a burden, but the sacrifice required to care for them can be a burden, especially when it catches you off guard. Fear regarding provision, which is often a concern, can distort our discernment when we are taking leaps. Remember—fear isn't a friend; it's a foe. We are allowed to feel the emotions that find themselves knocking at the door of our heart, but much like Nehemiah, we can't allow them to take up residence. Emotions should be our servants, not our masters. I once heard Pastor Rich Wilkerson Jr. say, "It's okay to not be okay; it's just not okay to stay that way."[2]

Although this leap comes with a lot of moving parts to consider, we must remember that God is not instructing us to do this leap alone. He is with us and will reveal more of His plans to us as we move along the path of obedience. And when it's time to return, similarly to when Nehemiah returned to his role as the king's cupbearer as we learn from Nehemiah 13:6, we should remember that this leap is only temporary, and we don't want to allow our assumptions about how the season *should* or *could* have been different to cause us to fall into condemnation or questioning.

REJECTING THE LIES

A few years ago, we decided to homeschool our two youngest children. As with any parental decision, it came with a lot of prayer, patience, and planning. At the time, we had three other children who were spread out between our local high school, middle school, and elementary school. However, we saw that the needs of our two youngest were a little different. We noticed our daughter's need for confidence and boldness within community and our son's need for monitoring until he grew out of his medical condition. We were moving away from the blended family services we'd previously offered and building a new brand-and-design business that focused on branding kingdom businesses and ministries. Because of these changes, we now had space in our lives to juggle homeschooling. We did that for three years—two on purpose and one on accident.

At the end of the second year of homeschooling, things had started to shift for me. My writing and speaking were taking off, and my children were ready to go into the classroom. I realized that God was leading me into a different season where I'd need more dedicated time in my day to effectively do everything well. As my husband and I talked through the changes, we agreed that it was time to send the kids to school. And that's when the lies started to run rampant.

Lies that said I was not putting my kids first.

Lies that said I was only thinking of myself.

Lies that said I wasn't doing what was best for them.

Lies that said I wasn't a good mother if my kids went back to school.

When we are being called to the Builder's Leap, lies can delay our return back into our initial assignment.

Lies that said sending them back would be failing them and my family.

Thankfully, my husband happens to be the modern-day Inspector Gadget and can quickly identify lies that the enemy is speaking to me. During that time, he would constantly remind me of the truth regarding our decision and God's plan for our children.

When we are being called to the Builder's Leap, lies can delay our return back into our initial assignment. Feelings of guilt, uncertainty, and shame might tempt us to, well, turn a pit stop into a permanent stop. I had to realize that God had temporarily called me to take on homeschooling for a very specific reason and season. God even graced us with another year to prepare ourselves and our children for the transition back to school, but it was still a difficult transition. For others, it might be a permanant way of life, but for us, it was only temporary, and I had to settle within myself that that was okay.

A little while after making the transition, I watched a message on YouTube that encouraged me. During the talk, panelist David Helm, who happened to be the only panelist who wasn't homeschooling and had children in the regular school system, was asked about the dangers of putting children in school and he shared this truth:

> The greatest dangers to our children are not outside. They're not external; they're internal. The greatest danger to the gospel lies within my own heart. And so that depth of understanding frees me to loose my children into the world upon the grace of God who will strengthen and ground them. . . .

Whatever decision you make for your children, make that decision in faith. It should be an act of faith, not fear . . . that God is going to grow your children no matter what."[3]

The Builder's Leap is one of the greatest opportunities to partner with God. We become the tangible hands and feet of Jesus as He uses us to bring forth His glory and story in the life of someone else, be it a child, a parent, or a friend. Through us, for a moment, they get to see a glimpse of the sacrificial nature of Jesus and His heart for them. What a great honor to serve God and people in that way.

CHAPTER 9

The Tentmaker's Leap

W hen my husband and I first started the ministry in 2016 that I shared about earlier, we were both working full-time jobs and raising our children. My husband was a property manager of a local housing agency, and I was a full-time high school teacher. We certainly already had a full plate as a blended family of nine, but we still felt God was nudging us to step out and start a ministry that would later serve blended families around the globe.

We'd both been raised in blended families and understood the dynamics surrounding them. As we brought our family together under one roof, we found ourselves navigating the challenging terrain of blending and knew we needed to intentionally build community and connection with others.

In the crevices of our busy life, we worked on creating resources to help other families. Also, our pastors at the time allowed us to lead a small group of blended-family couples at the church and test out some of the material we were producing. Somewhere along the way, what started out as a small group turned into a ministry that would have national and international reach.

For a couple years, we worked full-time during the day and spent evenings or weekends planning events, creating content, sharing on podcast and television interviews, managing blog contributors, conducting workshops, and more. Doing this was not an easy undertaking! It was a season when our willingness to say yes to God wasn't contingent on *convenience* but rather on *obedience*.

We could have both walked away from our jobs then to pursue the ministry full-time (which did eventually happen), but it wasn't quite time. God knew that we would need our full-time careers to help build the ministry. The cost of creating written resources, planning events, and operating a start-up ministry had to come from our personal funds until it was established and able to stand on its own.

We had to pray, press, and pay in order to see growth, but God provided.

Looking back, I realize that juggling full-time work, family, and ministry was what we had been called to do in that season. However, God equips those He calls, and He did just that for us. It was evident that our careers were a resource that God used to help fund our ministry and His mission, just like He did with the apostle Paul.

FROM TORMENTER TO TENTMAKER

Paul's conversion story in Acts 9 is one of several biblical narratives that allow us to meet the before-and-after version of an influential character.

Prior to Paul's transformation, his role as a Pharisee involved persecuting the church "violently" and trying to "destroy it" (Gal. 1:13). His conversion didn't mean that followers of Christ were immediately convinced that he was now *for* them instead of *against* them (see Acts 9:10–30). However, over time, it became clear that Paul was just as zealous a minister of the gospel as he was once a tormentor of God's people. His redirected zeal caused him to boldly preach the uncompromising good news of Jesus to those who were just as undeserving as he was. He even wrote several books in the New Testament and ushered the Gentiles into a revelation of Jesus, ultimately leading to the salvation of many. Paul went from being a persecutor of God's people to a mouthpiece for them.

Ministry became Paul's primary vocation while tentmaking became his trade of choice that helped support the mission of the ministry. We see this expressed in the book of Acts, first through his relationship with Aquila and Priscilla, then again when he was speaking to the Ephesian elders.

In Acts 18:1–3, we read:

> After this Paul left Athens and went to Corinth. And he found a Jew named Aquila, a native of Pontus, recently come from Italy with his wife Priscilla, because Claudius had commanded all the Jews to leave Rome. And he went to see them, and because he was of the same trade he stayed with them and worked, for they were tentmakers by trade.

This passage is followed by his conversation with the elders in Acts 20:33–35:

> "I coveted no one's silver or gold or apparel. You yourselves know that these hands ministered to my necessities and to those who were with me. In all things I have shown you that by working hard in this way we must help the weak and remember the words of the Lord Jesus, how he himself said, 'It is more blessed to give than to receive.'"

In both cases, we observe that Paul is dedicated to the ministry and can conclude that the income from his trade as a tentmaker helped to sustain it and him. In his case, like many of ours, it was a matter of "both-and" rather than "either-or."

THE DUAL-SERVICE PRINCIPLE

I love how the ministry Theology of Work explained Paul's ministry and monetary pursuit. In their article titled "Tent Making and Christian Life," they explain how tentmaking is a common metaphor used to describe Christians who work jobs that help support a "professional ministry":

> The term "bi-vocational" is often used to indicate that two separate professions are involved, the money-earning one and the ministry one. But Paul's example shows that all aspects of human life should be a seamless witness. There is little room to draw distinctions between "professional ministry" and other forms of witness. According to Acts, Christians actually have only one vocation . . . witnessing to the gospel. We have many forms of service, including preaching and pastoral care, making tents, building furniture, giving money and caring for the weak. A Christian who engages in a money-earning profession such as making tents, in order to support a non-money-earning profession such as teaching about Jesus, would be more accurately described as "dual service" rather than "bi-vocational"—one calling, two forms of service. The same would be true of any Christian who serves in more than one line of work.[1]

This description is powerful because it gives us permission to be missionally minded in any type of work we find ourselves doing. It also reveals that ministry is ongoing and aligns perfectly with what was described in an earlier chapter as *the* purpose.

When we want our ministry or business to be self-sufficient but it feels more like an expensive hobby, we can change our perspective and consider our work as one calling and two forms of service.

Our work, which we do "as for the Lord," (see Col. 3:23) isn't limited to a single occupation, but rather a singular storyline: the "on earth as it is in heaven" storyline (see Matt. 6:10). When we understand this truth, we don't feel pressed to choose between ministry and work. We can simply move as God leads, be it remaining on a job to build the ministry or leaving the job to focus on a ministry, business, or other endeavor. When this becomes the goal, it alleviates the pressure of trying to figure out "what" to do and helps us listen for "how" God wants it done.

> When we want our ministry or business to be self-sufficient but it feels more like an expensive hobby, we can change our perspective and consider our work as one calling and two forms of service.

THE MAKING OF A TENTMAKER

This leap is near and dear to my heart because it's the foremost leap I feel people struggle with being content in. I also feel it's one of the most common leaps people will encounter throughout their lifetime. I have met very few fishermen who weren't tentmakers first. The person called to the Tentmaker's Leap is being led to step out and start a ministry, business, or endeavor while still working in a job or career. Because of the dual nature of this leap, it requires a keen awareness and willingness to partner the job and God's calling together in the same season. It also requires strong community, delegation skills, and an understanding of what it means to co-labor with God and others.

Although this leap doesn't mean we will have to walk completely away from our job, it is often out of our comfort zone because it requires risk, trusting others, and sacrifice. As a tentmaker, we also need to be disciplined with our time as we balance identifying what to focus on and what to release to others.

Trusting God to build something from the ground up, even without the ability to be fully present in the process, demonstrates you may be a tentmaker.

If you find yourself in a tentmaker season, I want to encourage you to lean into godly wisdom and counsel as you learn to co-labor with God and others so that the work of the kingdom can go forth.

THE CO-LABORING CONUNDRUM

In case I've made writing a book seem easy, I want you to know it's not! As with any industry or career, writing has its set of difficulties, and while working on this book, I ran right into one of the greatest ones. I like to call it the "co-laboring conundrum"!

One day, while feeling completely overwhelmed with the progress—that I believed I *hadn't* made—and the time it was taking me to get the book done, I shared with my husband my frustration at myself. Granted, I still had seven months before the manuscript was due and I'd already completed over half the draft. However, I knew I hadn't met my personal deadline.

Can I just say this? Sometimes we're in competition with a version of ourselves that doesn't and can't exist—i.e., the sit-at-the-beach-with-a-cup-of-coffee-and-write-for-hours version of ourselves. *That* Rachel only exists in my mind right now—and possibly in a scrapbook if I cut out a picture of my head and put it on someone else's body that's at the beach! I've learned that we can go further faster if we become content and accept the present season of life when God calls us to leap. Maybe one day I'll be writing as I look at the sunrise on the beach, but right now, I'm writing before my kids wake up and I get them off to school, or while sitting in the car as I wait for the store to open, and that's quite all right. Getting the work done isn't always glamourous!

Now, let me get back to the original story. While I talked, my husband listened to me complain about my inability to meet the self-imposed deadline, schedule my time well, and create the way I desired. All those things, he later pointed out to me, were not accurate reflections of what I'd actually accomplished. But before he did that, he shared a perspective with me that shifted everything. He started by saying, "What if you're looking at this all wrong?"

He then began to explain how he saw my role as the author of this book as *part* of the co-laboring process with God for a book He wanted in the world. He mentioned that I was putting all this pressure on myself, as if there weren't others God had assigned to work alongside Him in this assignment.

The publisher, editors, designers, launch team, and marketing team all have necessary roles that were just as important to the book as mine as the author. He reminded me that, ultimately, this was an opportunity to be a co-laborer or fellow worker with God and others.

As a tentmaker, there are two types of co-laboring that we do: co-laboring with God (1 Cor. 3:9) and co-laboring with others (1 Cor. 12:14–29). Whenever you feel overwhelmed with trying to juggle everything, remember to step back and ask yourself, "Am I co-laboring with God and others or trying to do it all on my own?" And if you find that you are trying to do it alone, simply invite God and others back into the process. Remember, it's always better to do work *for* God *with* God.

CHAPTER 10

The Trailblazer's Leap

One day while dropping my children off at school, I was stopped by a lady I didn't know but who knew me. She introduced herself and started telling me how much of what I was doing was so similar to the work my mother did in her own ministry. She started to list the similarities she noticed—from writing and speaking to sharing on radio and television. She spoke about how my mother's ministry touched so many lives in the '80s and '90s. After she finished, I smiled and thanked her for sharing those stories with me.

I pondered what she told me for quite a while. That was several years ago, but that moment feels like yesterday.

I know without a doubt that my heart for ministry and my passion for people come from my mother and the work she did in the early years of my life. My older sister shared how she remembered my mom putting us in the car while my dad was at work and going to rescue a mother and her children from an abusive situation. I recall late nights in the Volkswagen as well but had no clue why we were in it. However, I do remember spending hours in her office as she typed on her typewriter and photocopied documents that she would later put in the file cabinet.

I was only six or seven years old during this time—too young to fully understand all that she was doing—but when someone would ask me what I wanted to be when I grew up, I would confidently say, "I want to be a minister."

I will always remember that season of my life because it embedded in my heart the seed of ministry that has flourished today. I'm thankful that my mother's ceiling became my floor and that she cleared the path in our family for me to confidently move forward in what God has called me to do for His glory.

This is what a trailblazer does; they clear the way for others that will come behind them, just as my mom did for me.

As we go into this final leap, I want to prepare you for a chapter that will flow a little differently from the previous chapters in this section. As you read it, try to see yourself as one who has been given a mandate to live a leaping lifestyle. You may not fully understand or embrace this request right now, but my hope is that by the end of the chapter, you will.

THE GREATEST LEAPER OF ALL TIME

While working through the leaps, I knew I needed to find a way to describe the person who has already done each of the other ones. *What do they do after that?*

I started to think of a biblical character whose life had been marked by a lifestyle of leaping. Almost immediately, the story of Jesus came to mind. His life was completely marked by His leaps. My mind began flooding with deeper revelation and insight as to how He demonstrated these in His earthly life. I thought about how Paul had the Tentmaker's Leap and Nehemiah had the Builder's Leap. *But how should I label Jesus' leap?*

In that moment, I did what I do whenever I get stumped—I asked my husband!

You weren't expecting me to say that now, were you?

After prayer, he is my go-to guy for figuring things out, so I explained to him my situation, and we started to brainstorm words that were in the Bible. However, nothing seemed to fit. That's when my husband mentioned the word "trailblazer," which surprisingly felt like the perfect description, and we both knew that was it! I grabbed my device too and we looked up the meaning of the word, which further confirmed our thoughts. It said, "one that blazes a trail to guide others."[1]

If you're thinking, *this fits perfectly, but when and how did He do the other leaps?*, keep reading; I'm about to teach you about the greatest leaper of all times.

FROM HEAVEN TO EARTH

In John 6, Jesus is talking to a crowd of followers about eternal life and true salvation. In this chapter, He says,

> "Truly, truly, I say to you, it was not Moses who gave you the bread from heaven, but my Father gives you the true bread from heaven. For the bread of God is he who comes down from heaven and gives life to the world." They said to him, "Sir, give us this bread always."
>
> Jesus said to them, "I am the bread of life; whoever comes to me shall not hunger, and whoever believes in me shall never thirst." (John 6:32–35)

Earlier, in John 3:13, Jesus tells Nicodemus, "No one has ascended into heaven except he who descended from heaven, the Son of Man."

These verses reveal the path and purpose of His Shepherd's Leap from heaven to earth. They show that He came by way of heaven to earth so that we may have eternal life through Him. His new location was right here with us and would be for thirty-three wonderful years.

Why is this significant?

Because for four hundred years, God didn't speak a word to His people. It was as if He'd said all there was to say to the previous generations. There were:

No pillars of cloud above guiding them.
No voice of a prophet warning them.
No angels appearing to them.
No leader being instructed by Him.
No miracles, signs, or wonders for them.
The silence echoed His Sovereignty.[2]

Then one day, an angel appeared to a young lady named Mary and revealed to her that she would deliver the Messiah, Immanuel—God with us—into the world. Her beautiful response is an indicator of her posture of obedience. "And Mary said, 'Behold, I am the servant of the Lord; let it be to me according to your word.' And the angel departed from her" (Luke 1:38).

Mary's willingness to remain pure and obedient allowed her to be used by God to bring our Savior into the world. This event was foretold by the prophet Isaiah, "Therefore the Lord himself will give you a sign. Behold, the virgin shall conceive and bear a son, and shall call his name Immanuel" (Isa. 7:14).

If you are like me, you may have read this Scripture before, understood its power, but never fully embraced the impact. A modern-day example—although it pales in comparison to what Christ did—is for the CEO of a multibillion-dollar company to *willingly* give up his role as CEO to become the janitor of *his* company.

Jesus' relocation into the world marked His Shepherd's Leap and began His journey into the Trailblazer's Leap. His willingness to become mankind *for* mankind is an act of love that may never fully be understood. Yet He didn't stop His leaps there; He continued in what we describe as the Tentmaker's Leap.

POWER AND POSITION

What if I told you that Jesus' Tentmaker's Leap didn't start with navigating carpentry and public ministry, although that is part of it? It actually started when He took on human form.

There could be no greater leap than the one we read about in John 1:1-4, 14:

> In the beginning was the Word, and the Word was with God, and the Word was God. He was in the beginning with God. All things were made through him, and without him was not any thing made that was made. In him was life, and the life was the light of men. . . .
>
> And the Word became flesh and dwelt among us, and we have seen his glory, glory as of the only Son from the Father, full of grace and truth.

That the Creator of all things loved us enough to die on the cross is unfathomable. But He became God with us.

Now, let's explore Jesus' Tentmaker's Leap from the perspective of Him as a carpenter and teacher. When Jesus became an adult, before going into full-time ministry, we see moments when He is asked to reveal His divine nature before His appointed time. An example of that moment is found in John 7:1–14, as He shares in a conversation with His brothers. Here's what takes place:

> After this Jesus went about in Galilee. He would not go about in Judea, because the Jews were seeking to kill him. Now the Jews' Feast of Booths was at hand. So his brothers said to him, "Leave here and go to Judea, that your disciples also may see the works you are doing. For no one works in secret if he seeks to be known openly. If you do these things, show yourself to the world." For not even his brothers believed in him. Jesus said to them, "My time has not yet come, but your time is always here. The world cannot hate you, but it hates me because I testify about it that its works are evil. You go up to the feast. I am not going up to this feast, for my time has not yet fully come." After saying this, he remained in Galilee.
>
> But after his brothers had gone up to the feast, then he also went up, not publicly but in private. The Jews were looking for him at the feast, and saying, "Where is he?" And there was much muttering about him among the people. While some said, "He is a good man," others said, "No, he is leading the people astray." Yet for fear of the Jews no one spoke openly of him. About the middle of the feast Jesus went up into the temple and began teaching.

Pay special attention to what Jesus tells His brothers. He tells them that His time had "not yet fully come." But it's also clear that He had performed miracles, taught in the synagogues, and revealed His divine nature to those closest to Him. His brothers were simply trying to silence the noise because when we are called to be ambassadors for Christ, there will be noise around us that tries to push us in one direction or another, prematurely.

The anointed time is the appointed time—and not a moment sooner.

But we must remember, just as Jesus did, that the anointed time is the appointed time—and not a moment sooner. This isn't easy, but as Jesus navigated the Tentmaker's Leap, He carried in His heart the desire for His greater assignment while He carried in His hand the tools to complete the current assignment; and for a season, He carried them both.

FROM FAMILY BUSINESS TO KINGDOM BUSINESS

Jesus spent His first thirty years of life preparing for His three years of full-time ministry. When the time finally came for Jesus' public ministry to begin, He went from full-time carpenter to tentmaker, then to focusing completely on the business of His heavenly Father.

During this Fisherman's Leap, He took the role of Savior very seriously, not allowing Himself to be deterred or distracted because He knew His mission was great and His time was limited. One day, His mother Mary called for Him while He was ministering and His response was, "'Who is my mother, and who are my brothers?' And stretching out his hand toward his disciples, he said, 'Here are my mother and my brothers! For whoever does the will of my Father in heaven is my brother and sister and mother'" (Matt. 12:48–50).

This may seem like a harsh response, but truly it was His way of letting everyone—including His family—know whose business He was helping to run now. He was no longer building His earthly father's carpentry business; He was now completely dedicated to

His heavenly Father's kingdom business. He was now on a mission to become the Savior of the world so His role as son to Mary no longer took priority.

During Jesus' Fisherman's Leap from carpenter to Savior, Jesus spent three of His thirty-three years on earth teaching, preaching, and performing miracles and healings to reveal He came to redeem us from the hand of death and bring us into salvation (John 3:17). Along the way, He came across doubters, demons, and danger, but He never lost sight of His ultimate goal of salvation of souls.

MISSION ACCOMPLISHED

After Jesus washed the disciples' feet, was betrayed by Judas, and was denied by Peter, Jesus shared some very important words with Thomas. In John 14:1–7, He says,

> "Let not your hearts be troubled. Believe in God; believe also in me. In my Father's house are many rooms. If it were not so, would I have told you that I go to prepare a place for you? And if I go and prepare a place for you, I will come again and will take you to myself, that where I am you may be also. And you know the way to where I am going." Thomas said to him, "Lord, we do not know where you are going. How can we know the way?" Jesus said to him, "I am the way, and the truth, and the life. No one comes to the Father except through me. If you had known me, you would have known my Father also. From now on you do know him and have seen him."

As the reader, we know what is about to happen next, but pretend for a moment that you don't know the end of this story. Imagine how Thomas felt as he heard these words. There's a chance he had begun to question everything he'd seen and believed over the last three years. He probably thought Jesus was immortal and invincible—which He was, but not for this occasion—and was shocked when Jesus spoke those words.

Jesus, however, knew His time was limited, so He warned the disciples and followers through parables and teachings during His three years of active ministry. This is one of the moments in Scripture where Jesus clearly expresses the temporary nature of His presence upon the earth, and we see the evidence of His Builder's Leap. He was telling Thomas that He wasn't going to be here long—that His time on earth was a temporary assignment, and He was going back to where He came from. Their inability to understand His assignment didn't change it.

He came because there was a need that went beyond our human ability to navigate. Humanity requires His help, and He wants our hearts. He came for us and to be with us because He loves us. This Builder's Leap serves as a lesson to us. Jesus' time on earth was temporary and reminds us that our time on earth is as well.

The astounding truth is that when we are in Christ, we are eternal ambassadors of heaven, while being temporary expatriates on earth. We are called to honor God through both our workings and our waiting, just as Jesus did!

THE MODERN-DAY TRAILBLAZER

People called to the Trailblazer's Leap often recognize that they have taken every other leap and are ready to lead others in their leaps. The evidence of this leap doesn't have to be extreme. For example, if you have ever walked away from your job or been let go, you're a fisherman. And realize that a move doesn't have to be across the country; it can be up the street or to college. If you've done this, you've taken the Shepherd's Leap. Or maybe you were temporarily laid off from your job but chose to use that time to start your ministry or write a book, and then when a position opened back up, you went back into the career—that would mean you've done the Builder's Leap. If you're taking courses on how to do something that you're passionate about that doesn't relate to your career—well, that's right in the zone of a tentmaker. Most of us *are* trailblazers and don't even realize it. Consider the small things you have done that would count as any of these leaps.

> The trailblazer's perspective has changed from *Why me?* to *Wow, me?* as they now understand the glory and power that God releases to those who obey His commands and live out His plans.

The main point is that a trailblazer recognizes and understands that we live a leaping lifestyle, and this person has learned to choose obedience to God over comfort and complacency. The trailblazer has already done all four of the other leaps in some capacity, and they're now able to lead the way for other people who God wants to lead into new seasons of transition. Their experiences have caused them to build trust in God's process and His plan, and they are willing to share their story to help others.

Although they are still making leaps themselves because it's a lifestyle, they have come to embrace the journey rather than reject it. Their perspective has changed from *Why me?* to *Wow, me?* as they now understand the glory and power that God releases to those who obey His commands and live out His plans. With a surrendered life and a willing heart, they confidently and boldly step into unknown, uncomfortable, and unfamiliar territory with God and watch as He becomes the lamp unto their feet and light unto their path. Additionally, they graciously mentor others to do the same.

This is the path of the trailblazer; if that's you, well done! Now, onward and upward we go.

Your Leaping Path

CHAPTER 11

Your Prayer Plan

W hen God begins to show us glimpses of how He would like to use our lives, it can be intimidating, but it doesn't have to be.

It can be easy to minimize the wonderful honor that we have to converse with God at any given moment of the day. We should consider it a remarkable opportunity to adventure and strategize with the Creator of the world. However, sometimes knowing how to do this can get a little overwhelming.

I've spent a significant part of my life as a Christ follower. In my late teens and early twenties, I slipped away for a bit but quickly came back to Christ when my circumstances became less than what I knew God desired for me.

In all those years, I had been taught many things about prayer. My father was a strong intercessor with a passion for prayer. It was never a shock to wake up in the early hours of the morning and find my father sitting in the chair praying before he headed off to work. This was his posture in the morning and before he went to bed at night. I was certain to be a natural prayer warrior, or so you'd think. Yet in my early thirties, I was confronted with a painful reality: I didn't know how to pray.

At least not the right way.

Based on all the things I had learned about prayer, it seemed that I had been doing everything wrong.

Pray on your knees; don't stand up.

Pray in this order; say this first.

Close your eyes; keep your eyes open.

Put your head down; hold it up.

Start the prayer like this; end the prayer like that.

Eventually, I found myself wanting to pray but feeling like I didn't know how. It was complicated and confusing, and I didn't want to say or do the wrong thing to mess up my chances of God hearing my prayer out of all the millions of prayers in the world. If I got it just right, maybe He would hear it and my prayer would be chosen as the winning prayer for the day.

That sounds ridiculous, but with all these perceived rules of praying, that is how I felt. It was as if prayer was part of a daily drawing of some sort, and if I followed all the rules, mine would get selected.

The realization of my prayer struggle happened one day when I needed to get through to God and found myself stalling. I wasn't confident that my prayers were good enough. I couldn't remember all the rules and would have certainly failed all the prerequisites for saying the perfect prayer. I was tired of calling others and asking them to pray for me when I knew I could pray for myself if I could just figure out how to cut through the red tape. What was I to do?[1]

That's when I learned that prayer is a conversation with God. It's approaching Him with honor, not perfection. It's a conversation between two of the most important people to each other, a Creator and His creation.

If what God shows you begins to feel too big, tell Him in prayer how you feel. If it feels inconvenient, tell Him that too. If it feels impossible, share your heart about that in prayer.

We pray not because He will change what He has requested us to do, but because He can change our belief surrounding the feelings we have developed from His request. He can even remind us of when we had those same feelings in the past and how He walked with us through those moments.

Here is the other thing I love about prayer: it is a two-way conversation. Hearing God's response in my life often happens through a thought that drops in my mind while I'm reading the Word or praying. Other times it's a gentle whisper or a warning revealing that my heart posture is in need of realignment. And other times it's a part of a Scripture that seems fitting for the conversation, and when I look up the remaining part, it is exactly what I needed to know and read.

When we become silent and listen, God will speak to us very specifically. It is during this time that we will receive a strategy for the vision He has given us. He may tell us lots of detail or the immediate next step, depending on how much we can handle, as we live and leap.

TEACH ME HOW TO PRAY

In Luke 11, we are met with a request that Jesus not only answers straightforwardly for His disciples, but through parables, for context and greater understanding. My desire is not to provide you with another prayer formula but to teach you about the nature of God as a friend and Father through these passages of Scripture.

In Luke 11:1–4 it says,

Now Jesus was praying in a certain place, and when he finished, one of his disciples said to him, "Lord, teach us to pray, as John taught his disciples." And he said to them, "When you pray, say:

"Father, hallowed be your name.

Your kingdom come.

Give us each day our daily bread,

and forgive us our sins,

for we ourselves forgive everyone who is indebted to us.

And lead us not into temptation."

If you're like me, you've heard this prayer hundreds, if not thousands, of times, but I want you to explore a little deeper into this moment between Jesus and His disciples. Although we don't know where Jesus was every single instance He chose to pray to His heavenly Father, we know that His life of prayer had piqued the interest of His disciples. At the time of this request, they'd already seen Him perform miracles, signs, and wonders and had even been sent out to perform some themselves (see Luke 9:1–6).

Jesus—who'd already proven His power and wisdom when He calmed storms, gave life-changing sermons, and raised people from the dead—was now being asked a question that would create a bridge of communication between heaven and earth. Suddenly, after all these significant moments, the disciples paused to consider the priority and power of prayer. It was as if they realized that they could experience and perform all these amazing works, but apart from prayer, they wouldn't have the connection with God the Father that Jesus had.

Has this ever happened to you? Have you ever been busy working—be it in the ministry, marketplace, or home—and the work you are doing is glorious but there is still a longing in your soul? It's like you know something is missing in your walk with Christ, although you can't put your finger on what it is. Then someone comes along, and you realize that what you're missing is a deeper experience similar to what you see them encountering in their walk with Christ. It's not in a covetous way but in an invitational way—as if God is saying He wants this with you and more.

Not only does He want our tasks and to-do lists; He wants our time. He doesn't want us simply doing things for Him; He wants us to do it with Him. I have fallen into the trap many times of doing things for God and missing the opportunity to do things with God. It's a constant battle I work to overcome. I've heard two amazing people speak on this concept of doing things with God versus for God—author Shae Bynes and YouTube influencer Daniel Kwak.

> God doesn't want us simply doing things for Him; He wants us to do it with Him.

Both brought great perspective and insight to this idea. All in all, I believe the disciples noticed how they were being empowered to do things for God but missing the opportunity to do things with God, and prayer was the key that would create the change.

When the disciples finally asked Jesus about prayer, He didn't say, "Well, it's about time you asked," or, "You all aren't anointed enough to do this yet. Maybe after you deny Me and I forgive you, you can pray to My Father." Maybe by our self-righteous standards, He would have had every reason to say all of the above and more—knowing what He knew was to come. But instead, He simply responded with a prayer that has served as a model for centuries, pointing to how we can approach the throne of grace—the prayer that we now call "The Lord's Prayer."

SPIRITUAL SENSITIVITY

When it comes to leaping, prayer is the primary ingredient that will facilitate God's will on earth and not our own. I've come to realize that there are typically six areas we tend to cover concerning prayer: who, what, where, when, why, how. In the English language, this is known as the Kipling Method. Now, we may not be completely aware that we are doing this when we are about to pray; however, they are each important to consider at some point, especially if we find ourselves stuck in our prayer time.

As you begin your prayer time, you may ask yourself:

1. Who am I praying for?
2. What am I praying about? What am I praying for?
3. Where do I see someone in the Bible with a similar prayer request? Where is it easiest for me to pray in quiet?
4. When should I start or stop praying about this? When is the best time of day for me to have dedicated prayer time?
5. Why do I need to pray about this?
6. How should I approach prayer regarding this matter? How often/long should I labor in prayer about it?

My goal here isn't to give you a "prayer formula" but rather to have you consider these things as you go into prayer so that God can speak to you on the matters as you pray. For example, there have been times when a person or situation would come to my mind, and my first thought would be, *Let me call them or see what's going on with that*. Then, after eventually getting around to calling them, I realized that what God was prompting me to do was pray for that person or situation at that moment. The more prayer became second nature, the more I was given to pray about.

When we respond in prayer, we can react on purpose. Through prayer, God may lead us to call them and encourage them, send them a direct message on social media that hits their inbox at the perfect moment, stop by right when they need someone to talk to, send them a resource we come across that we didn't even know they needed, or some other reaction that couldn't have been predetermined. His sovereignty will guide us if we choose to be spiritually sensitive to His leading, and this sensitivity to prayer will also help to propel us and others into a leap God is calling us to take.

FRIEND AND FATHER

In the verses following the Lord's Prayer, we find a parable about friendship that Jesus shares with His disciples. This parable is intended to give us a deeper look into God's heart surrounding prayer and answered prayers.

Generally speaking, men and women approach friendship very differently. Women often look for the emotional and lifestyle connections, while men tend to be drawn to more positional and professional friendships. In either case, we all carry expectations within our friendships because the role of friend holds a strong and important place in our lives. Understanding these distinct differences and shifting our perspective to interpret this parable through the lens of Christ gives us the greatest opportunity to learn what God intended from this story.

Jesus knew well how important friendship is in life and expressed His heart toward prayer through the lens of this relationship. He begins in Luke 11:5–8 by setting the stage for an expectation we might have of a close friend when we are in a moment of need.

And he said to them, "Which of you who has a friend will go to him at midnight and say to him, 'Friend, lend me three loaves, for a friend of mine has arrived on a journey, and I have nothing to set before him'; and he will answer from within, 'Do not bother me; the door is now shut, and my children are with me in bed. I cannot get up and give you anything'? I tell you, though he will not get up and give him anything because he is his friend, yet because of his impudence he will rise and give him whatever he needs."

This parable is in regard to the disciples asking Jesus to teach them how to pray. It may seem odd at first, but what Jesus is doing here is answering their question, as well as the question behind the question which is, "What if God doesn't answer my prayer?" He is acknowledging that there are times when we might pray for something and not get the answer we want right away. But our persistence in asking will move the heart of God—like it did the friend—to move on our behalf. He is saying that when we need something, if we keep asking, we will receive it in His time and in His way.

This reminds me of my first son. He is persistent in every way. I might say he gets his persistence from me—I mean, I am the girl who knocked on the elementary school door every day during the summer of my fourth grade to remind the secretary that I wanted a very special teacher to be my fifth-grade teacher! All I know is that when my son realized that if he kept asking me something over and over I would eventually tell him yes, he took that and ran with it. Of course, there are times I am adamant and say no, and he doesn't always agree or understand those times. However, when I say yes to something I've been saying no to, his persistence usually plays a huge role in that change of heart!

God wants us to be the same way in prayer, which is what He is explaining in this parable. He ends His conversation about this topic with the disciples in Luke 11 by saying this,

"And I tell you, ask, and it will be given to you; seek, and you will find; knock, and it will be opened to you. For everyone who asks receives, and the one who seeks finds, and to the one who knocks it will be opened. What father among you, if his son asks for a fish, will instead of a fish give him a serpent; or if he asks for an egg, will give him a scorpion? If you then, who are evil, know how to give good gifts to your children, how much more will the heavenly Father give the Holy Spirit to those who ask him!" (Luke 11:9–13)

THE ARMOR AND PRAYER

As we prepare to leap, there will be many things that happen along the way—some good and others challenging. We have talked about this throughout the book. However, I want to warn you that your obedience will attract opposition, just like with Nehemiah. Unexpected hurdles and unfortunate life interruptions will happen despite our pursuit toward God's will in our lives. I like to say that life is going to keep on living—that's all it knows to do and what it does best. That is why we must remind ourselves to prepare for war in the spirit as we wait for God's preordained and predestined plans to unfold in the natural. When heaven touches earth through our obedience, the enemy isn't happy, but it doesn't change the fact that he is still defeated.

So how do we prepare for war? You may already have some insight into this, but, as always, I want you to take a deeper look with me. Let's look at the familiar passage of Scripture in Ephesians 6:14–17 about the armor that God provides:

> Stand therefore, having fastened on the belt of truth, and having put on the breastplate of righteousness, and, as shoes for your feet, having put on the readiness given by the gospel of peace. In all circumstances take up the shield of faith, with which you can extinguish all the flaming darts of the evil one; and take the helmet of salvation, and the sword of the Spirit, which is the word of God.

With this armor, God has given us everything we need to fight and win the attacks that come against us. However, what we don't see as part of the armor is prayer. Why wouldn't prayer be a piece of the armor? It seems just as important as faith, truth, and the Word of God. Had the writer of Ephesians forgotten to add that part of the armor? Absolutely not. Prayer is so important to war against the enemy that it can be found apart from the uniform while still essential to winning the battle. Read what it says in verse 18 right after the verses that speak of the armor: "Praying at all times in the Spirit, with all prayer and supplication. To that end, keep alert with all perseverance, making supplication for all the saints."

Prayer produces an environment that makes the armor effective. It is through prayer that we become alert and can fight effectively as the fiery darts are thrown at us. Every leap is intended to prepare us to make God's name great all over the earth, beginning in the places and spaces He chooses to send us. Satan's darts are his attempt to hinder or stop our progress, but it's our prayers that help us persevere and that move us forward to victory. Remember, it is he who endures until the end that will be saved (Matt. 24:13), and with the armor and prayer, we can endure for the sake of the gospel.

A HOLY INVITATION

As we end this chapter, I want to take a moment and encourage you with a prayer. Living a leaping lifestyle can be an overwhelming adventure, especially when we don't see the evidence of God's presence and guidance. Without these, we will second-guess our decisions, stall in fear, and question our motives. I know because I've been there and still struggle in these areas. But I've also found that when we saturate our decision in prayer, we can see the hand of God moving in unimaginable ways and in His perfect timing.

Our leaps are truly invitations from God, the Creator of heaven and earth, to partner with Him. It's the same invitation God gave the Israelites when they left Egypt, Ruth when she chose not to return to her family of origin, and Jonah when he finally chose obedience rather than dismay. It's an invitation to enter into a promised place and position with God. Anything we do with God comes with a guarantee: it will turn out for our good (Rom. 8:28)!

Let us pray.

Dear heavenly Father,

As I come humbly before Your throne of grace, I first repent for my disobedience, doubting, and fear. I repent for not moving when You told me to move and not trusting You completely for the good plans You have for my life. I thank You for Your Son, Jesus Christ, who died for my sins, and I receive Your forgiveness of sins and salvation.

Lord, as I begin my journey of leaping with You, I have many things pressing on my heart. Some concerns, some uncertainties, and some false beliefs. God, I ask that You would clear the path of lies and lead me down the path of truth, daily. I thank You for choosing me to become the evidence of Your love for others through this leap because I know that my leap is connected to someone else's future. I pray that as You make the path clear and straight, I would keep my eyes on You. Not on my current circumstances, not on the impossibilities, but completely on You. Let Your voice become the loudest, most gentle voice in my head as I move forward in Your will.

Lord, let me be a lamp that stands on a hill and shines bright for others to see Your goodness through this act of faith, that You might be glorified in and through me.

In Jesus' name,
Amen

CHAPTER 12

Your Posture of Preparation

I n all of middle and most of high school, I played the flute in the school band. I loved it! Unfortunately, I made it through *one* band camp and quickly realized that I was not cut out for the camp luxuries of early-morning marching in mud, stale food, and community bathrooms. However, I was dedicated to playing the flute and quite good at it, often being first or second chair in band. Because of my growing skill level, one day the band teacher invited me to compete in a regional competition. I was thrilled, but preparing for those competitions was gruesome—and I thought camp was uncomfortable!

I'd spend hours on end in my bedroom or the band room practicing the song I had chosen for the competition. Anyone who has played in band knows that the room becomes a home away from home (or better yet, class away from class). But if you are preparing to compete, your whole life revolves around that moment. You eat, sleep, and breathe the notes and music sheet. That was me.

When competition day finally arrived, the school bus dropped us off early in the morning to the location that was sponsoring that year's event. I remember roaming the halls of this unfamiliar school with the other students who were competing from my school, trying to find a place to sit and relax until our time came to compete. Every person from each school was assigned a classroom and competition number. The band teachers didn't receive their students' information until the day of the event, so we had to arrive early—even if we didn't compete until late afternoon—so no one would miss his or her turn. Everyone was scheduled for a different time throughout the day, and possibly in a different classroom, depending on your instrument.

When my turn finally came, I remember going to the classroom early and waiting outside the door until the person before me finished. My teacher was with me, and when they finally called my name, I walked in, placed my music on the stand, answered a few preliminary questions, and started to play. My fingers moved at the speed of light to make sure each note came out precisely. I balanced the air that flowed into the flute so that the sound was just right. And once the song ended, I rested my fingers while my heart beat quickly, awaiting the next steps. The song I'd practiced for hours, weeks, and months lasted for about two to three minutes.

I know you're wondering: *Well, did you win?* I'd say yes, although I don't recall walking away with a prize. Honestly, I don't remember what happened, but I know I didn't leave the school in tears so I must have gotten something for my hours of labor, or I was hurt so terribly by the unexpected loss that I can't remember. I'll choose the first memory. Unfortunately, if you were to ask me to play the flute today, you would be sadly disappointed. The only thing I can play now is the B scale (if that's even what it's called) and some other scale. Nonetheless, I learned a valuable lesson about preparation during that season of my life: we will often spend more time preparing for the moment than the moment itself actually requires. However, much like with Bezalel, those moments in history truly create His-story in our lives.

BEZALEL'S POSTURE OF PREPARATION

As we read through the book of Exodus, we are met with many significant moments surrounding the Israelites' lifestyle of worship, sacrifice, and consecration unto God. As God begins to lead them toward their promised position in Him, He starts by establishing laws (known as the Ten Commandments), anointing the people who would lead, and building the place where His presence could reside among them. This place was known as the tabernacle, the place that would house His glory.

It was intended to be symbolic of His presence, holiness, and laws.

And before the beginning of time, God had already chosen who would be assigned as the person to build the tabernacle, as well as its accompanying ark of the covenant, altar, and priestly garments. His name was Bezalel.

Let's see exactly what the Bible says about Bezalel.

The LORD said to Moses, "See, I have called by name Bezalel the son of Uri, son of Hur, of the tribe of Judah, and I have filled him with the Spirit of God, with ability and intelligence, with knowledge and all craftsmanship, to devise artistic designs, to work in gold, silver, and bronze, in cutting stones for setting, and in carving wood, to work in every craft. And behold, I have appointed with him Oholiab, the son of Ahisamach, of the tribe of Dan. And I have given to all able men ability, that they may make all that I have commanded you." (Ex. 31:1–6)

When I first read this passage of Scripture, I'd been reading through Exodus for about a month. Up until then, I didn't understand the level of involvement Bezalel had in this project given to Moses. If there is one thing that stood out to me as I read, it was when the Lord said, "See, I have called by name Bezalel the son of Uri."

Ponder with me for a moment. Do you realize how significant it is to be chosen by God to do such a monumental task? Do you recognize that you, too, have been chosen before the beginning of time to posture yourself for a moment just as significant as this one? Although your moment may not be building a tabernacle or creating the priestly garments, your moment is just as significant because it will impact the world and all of eternity if you choose to obey.

It's one thing to be called, but it's a whole other thing to be called by name. How humbling it must have been for Bezalel to know that Moses and God were having a conversation about him. God was informing Moses of what was to be done and who was going to lead in doing it. This is so much like the nature of God—to make one person aware that there is work that needs to be done and bring the names of others to their attention as someone who can get it done. He has a wonderful way of aligning His will with our skill.

This divine networking has happened to me more than once. Oftentimes, there are jobs that have never been on my radar that someone thought I might be qualified for or interested in, and they turned out to be a wonderful fit. Other times, I've spoken with event planners who said my name came up during a meeting and it gave me the opportunity to share a powerful message as a keynote for their event. At times, influential people had conversations about me where I know it was God who brought me into the conversation! It's an honor to know God is leading others to see my skills and giftings and allowing me to lead.

It also reminds me of some wise words my dad would always tell me when I was a teenager, "Your reputation goes farther than you do!" Now that I'm an adult, I totally understand what he meant by that, and I repeat it to my children all the time. Bezelal, the craftsman, experienced that truth firsthand. His God-given skill as a craftsman would enable him to produce great work for God's glory on earth—what an honor!

It isn't until Exodus 35 that Bezalel and the people of Israel become aware of the request that God has made to Moses about Bezalel. Let's take a look (it may sound very familiar):

> Then Moses said to the people of Israel, "See, the LORD has called by name Bezalel the son of Uri, son of Hur, of the tribe of Judah; and he has filled him with the Spirit of God, with skill, with intelligence, with knowledge, and with all crafts-manship, to devise artistic designs, to work in gold and silver and bronze, in cutting stones for setting, and in carving wood, for work in every skilled craft. And he has inspired him to teach, both him and Oholiab the son of Ahisamach of the tribe of Dan" (Ex. 35:30–34).

Do we know if Bezalel knew that God was going to call him to this great work when he was spending time becoming skilled? No, we are not given a timeline. However, we do know that Bezalel was prepared (skilled) and *inspired* to teach others who would later work alongside him. Through this, they would all be prepared for the moment they were called upon by God to build the tabernacle.

We don't know what transpired in his life after that major assignment; however, we do know that moment made history and His-story.

LEADING AND LEANING

What is a posture of preparation?

It's being ready for *what* God wants to do and *when* He wants to do it in our lives. It's when our willingness and God's will create an on-earth-as-it-is-in-heaven moment.

It's a settling in our minds and hearts of what it means to say, "Not my will, Lord, but Yours be done."

And it's doing whatever we can to be ready for His request but not feeling unqualified to accept if things aren't perfect when He calls us.

Being prepared isn't always easy. It sometimes means we're doing things in a season, and we have no clue why.

Working a job that doesn't seem at all related to our future plans or goals may have us wondering if we are in the right place and doing the right thing, but we can be confident in His plans to work everything together for our good.

Maybe walking away from your career to help a family member who seemed unappreciative or confrontational about your sacrifice has you confused as to whether the investment was worthwhile, but know that your willingness and sacrifice didn't go unseen by God.

Seasons of preparation can leave us wondering: *What was the point of that season? What did it contribute to God's plan for my life?*

I've been there. I recall a season not too long ago when I struggled to find work. I wanted to be home when my children came home, and I was homeschooling our youngest. Unfortunately, our bills exceeded what was in our bank account, and to make ends meet, my husband and I took work in food and grocery delivery.

It was a humbling season to say the least. Dreading the thought of delivering food to someone I knew and trying to figure out what I'd say to them if they saw me left me with some anxiety. I remember thinking, *I have a master's degree and have coached people who make six and seven figures. How did I end up here?*

I'm sure I verbalized my struggles a few times to my husband (whose ego has never stopped him from taking care of his family, and for that I am thankful). I couldn't imagine how that difficult season was going to help me in my pursuit as an entrepreneur and ministry leader. It just wasn't making sense at all.

Can you guess what God showed me? Even in that uncomfortable season, He was leading me every step of the way and posturing me for His promises. Beside the fact that I needed a dose of humility, He knew I needed to understand and become more empathetic. With fresh eyes, I could see those whose road to His will wasn't paved with ease and simplicity, whose life didn't look like it was marked by success but rather striving and struggle. My posture of leaning into the uncomfortable seasons gave Him permission to lead me into deeper compassion and care for those in a similar season.

Romans 8:28 speaks beautifully into this place of leaning and leading. It says, "And we know that for those who love God all things work together for good, for those who are called according to his purpose."

This reminder reveals that all things work together according to His purpose, not ours. And that's what a posture of preparation always keeps in mind.

THE POSTURE OF REST

It's not easy to die to the desires of flesh. Our flesh is always after comfort and carefree living rather than the hope of glory that the spirit longs for. Paul said it best when he said, "For to me to live is Christ, and to die is gain" (Phil. 1:21). I've learned that "to live is Christ" is to accomplish His will upon the earth. Each day is an opportunity to do just that.

No matter what God is using to accomplish His will, a posture of preparation is always accompanied by a posture of rest.

This opportunity may come packaged as a willingness to transition to a new role at your job even when it doesn't seem like a logical idea. Or maybe choosing to take a leave of absence to work on a heart-passion project is the opportunity. It may even be having a degree that could be used to serve an industry but instead using it to serve your children as a homeschool mom.

No matter what God is using to accomplish His will, a posture of preparation is always accompanied by a posture of rest.

As we continue in Exodus 31 referenced earlier, we see that God prepares the people for the work, requirements, and sacrifices they will need in building the tabernacle. In verses 12–18, however, He reminds them that even in doing something for God (building the tabernacle), the Sabbath must be honored and kept holy. He wasn't changing His Ten Commandments even though the work to be done was a holy tabernacle. Rest was required for work; it was not optional. It served as a posture of honor and trust in the God who sent them to do the work. From this, we might gather that a posture of rest is even more honoring to God than work because it places us back at the feet of Jesus and reminds us that we are co-laborers with Him, not independent workers.

Our resistance to rest often comes from a posture of performance rather than surrender and submission. Rest reinforces that we are earthly beings that have been invited to partner with God's heavenly will. We are not machines or robots; we are sons and daughters who can take a day and be with Him—basking in the fullness of His presence and trusting in the finished work He will accomplish through us. We can rest because He is God, and we are not. God promises that His yoke is easy and His burden is light, and we can trust His word. He says in Matthew 11:28–30, "Come to me, all who labor and are heavy laden, and I will give you rest. Take my yoke upon you, and learn from me, for I am gentle and lowly in heart, and you will find rest for your souls. For my yoke is easy, and my burden is light."

As we posture ourselves through preparation, let's not forget to honor God with our posture of rest.

CHAPTER 13

Your Petition

My not-yet-preteen youngest daughter has been on a mission since she was about three years old. She has wanted a cellphone. I don't know who she imagined she'd be calling on it at such a young age, but she must have had a list of people who were expecting to hear from her to have such a "need."

Now, this is not a discussion about whether a child should or shouldn't have a cellphone; I will leave that to each parent's discretion. However, my husband and I decided some time ago that we weren't getting our youngest two children cellphones until they were in extracurricular activities without our presence. Since we take them to school less than sixty seconds away from the house, pick them up, transport them to sports practices, sit with them, bring them home, and live with them, it just didn't seem like a necessary bill. To add to the list, the teachers don't allow cellphones in the classroom due to the distractions they can cause to the students. Although my daughter feels a need for a cellphone since most of her friends have them, she finds ways to communicate with us through the school email or by calling us on a friend's phone—often with minor needs or wants.

Nonetheless, the other day when I went over to my office desk, I noticed a half piece of paper sitting where my computer usually sits. I sat down and grabbed the paper and started to read it. It was a letter from Gabby titled, "Why I should have a cellphone when I turn 13." The length of the note surprised me. I didn't realize she could type so much already. I knew she must have taken some time and had thought through her points. Since she still had a few years to go before the appointed age, I had some time to take them into consideration.

Now I could have come up with tons of reasons why she shouldn't have a cellphone, but I wasn't going to dampen her spirits. As I read through the note, I paid attention to how intentional she had been with addressing many of our concerns while bringing attention to things she assumed we hadn't considered. She mentioned her older siblings having cellphones, her need to stay in contact with us when she was away from the house, and she even provided specific phones that were kid-friendly and could provide us control and comfort. She was thorough, her writing was impressive, and she presented a strong case for only being ten. My husband and I have walked this road five times already, but I'm certainly proud of her for overcoming her fear, advocating for her future, and petitioning for what she wanted.

PLANNING TO PETITION

Petitions are powerful tools that bring to light problems, concerns, and needs. *Merriam-Webster* states that a petition is "a formal written request made to an authority or organized body (such as a court)."[1] When taking leaps, petitions are part of the process and help to clear the pathway as we walk in obedience. This reminds me of what Nehemiah had to do in order to fulfill his mission of rebuilding the wall.

Once Nehemiah was presented with the condition of the wall, there were several things he had to do in order to prepare for the journey ahead of rebuilding it. The time between receiving the information from his brother and setting out to do the work entailed prayer, preparation, and planning. Some of that preparation would be done in the form of a petition.

After the king approved Nehemiah's request to go to Jerusalem and help his people, Nehemiah needed the king to do a few more things to make the mission successful. Here is how he presented his additional request to the king:

> And I said to the king, "If it pleases the king, let letters be given me to the governors of the province Beyond the River, that they may let me pass through until I come to Judah, and a letter to Asaph, the keeper of the king's forest, that he may give me timber to make beams for the gates of the fortress of the temple, and for the wall of the city, and for the house that I shall occupy." And the king granted me what I asked, for the good hand of my God was upon me. (Neh. 2:7–8)

There are a few things we can learn from Nehemiah in this exchange with the king with regard to planning and petitioning:

Do the Research

Nehemiah knew exactly what was ahead of him and what he would need to pass through to the other side. He had already done the research while he was waiting for the opportunity to present itself. Nehemiah was thorough and knew who he would need to talk to, what he would need to ask for, and how long he would be gone. He didn't know everything he would encounter along the way, but he used what he did know to prepare for the unknowns.

Always Be Ready

Nehemiah likely had no clue when he would be able to talk to the king about the matter, but he lived in preparedness for when the time came. He had everything he needed. He didn't walk away and then come back another day to say, "Oh, dear King, by the way. I totally forgot that I'm going to need this document signed and this permission given as well." No, he was ready when the moment came and with research diligently done beforehand.

Face the Fear

When we examine a few verses prior to verses 7 and 8, we see, "And the king said to me, 'Why is your face sad, seeing you are not sick? This is nothing but sadness of the heart.' Then I was very much afraid" (Neh. 2:2). Nehemiah was afraid of the leap he was about to make. Speaking to the king could get him killed; he wasn't even allowed to look sad in the king's presence,[2] much less make such a bold request. However, his obedience to God and his desire for the future to look different from the past gave him courage to do something hard in order to accomplish something good.

Nehemiah's petition gave him the access he needed to begin the journey with a solid plan. He took the time to define the order and structure of what would need to be done before beginning his mission. Although he didn't have control over all the variables, he was prepared for many of them. Nehemiah in the Old Testament teaches us through his obedience and petition about a concept that Jesus reveals in the New Testament—what it means to count the cost.

COUNT THE COST

One day while Jesus talked to a crowd about bearing their cross and following Him, He shared an analogy that I believe is significant when we are taking leaps that require us to petition.

"For which of you, desiring to build a tower, does not first sit down and count the cost, whether he has enough to complete it? Otherwise, when he has laid a foundation and is not able to finish, all who see it begin to mock him, saying, 'This man began to build and was not able to finish.' Or what king, going out to encounter another king in war, will not sit down first and deliberate whether he is able with ten thousand to meet him who comes against him with twenty thousand? And if not, while the other is yet a great way off, he sends a delegation and asks for terms of peace." (Luke 14:28–32)

Jesus used the examples of building a tower and going to war to explain that before choosing to be His disciple, a person needed to count the cost. Similarly, every decision we make, including choosing to leap, will have an impact—make sure this is what you really want to do before you do it. Also, consider the totality of what you are agreeing to before you start.

There is a correlation between the opening story of my daughter, Nehemiah, and Jesus' conversation with the crowd: they all point back to counting the cost. My daughter wanted my husband and me to be aware of the cost of her not having a cellphone, so she submitted a request to us including specific information. Nehemiah counted the cost of going to the king unprepared versus having his petitions ready, which would set him up for greater success. And Jesus shifts His conversation with the crowd from a parable about a celebration feast (see Luke 14:12–24) to counting the cost of their decision to follow Him.

From these three scenarios, we can conclude something about counting the cost—it's ultimately about our now and later.

FROM NOW TO LATER

The decisions we make now will benefit or harm our future, which is our later. Think about choices you've made in the past and afterward said to yourself, *If only I hadn't done that.* Conversely, consider the situations where you have thought, *Wow, what a blessing that I decided to do that anyway!* I know I have made this statement more than once: *If only I knew then what I know now.* There is a now-and-later effect to everything we choose to do or not do. Learning to count the cost gives us the opportunity to be prepared rather than be caught off guard, much like Brandi did in chapter 7 when choosing to move from Memphis to Washington.

In God's economy, waiting means being obedient and productive.

I always remind myself that God won't give me the next set of instructions for my life until I'm obedient to the last (or present) set that He has already given me. This is because by being obedient to the last set of instructions, I'm often prepared and positioned to receive the next. It's as if my obedience is part of my counting the cost.

Remember, waiting in God's kingdom is an action word, unlike in our world in which waiting often lends itself to the idea of sitting still. In God's economy, waiting means being obedient and productive. God doesn't want us waiting idly but rather actively because there is always a bridge between now and later.

Here's what counting the cost and actively waiting in obedience may look like for you:

Researching houses and the housing market

Getting résumé help

Working on your credit rating

Obtaining a certification or degree

Seeking childcare support

Looking into new church homes to visit

Starting the ministry or business with your own funds

Getting guidance on how to write a grant or book

Investing in coaching, conferences, or collaborations

Taking a class to strengthen your skills

The list could go on and on. Only you know what you need to do next for the leap God has given you and who you need to connect with to make the process smooth.

BUT WHAT IF?

As I wrote out this list, I could already hear some of you saying, "But what if _____?" (you can fill in the blank).

What if I don't have the funds to start the business or take the class?

What if no one will watch my children while I work on that project?

What if I don't have the time or resources?

What if I do all this work and it fails?

Although all of these reasons are legitimate obstacles, they only become barriers if we lose sight of who called us to the work. I want to remind you that we are not responsible for the outcome;

you are, however, responsible for obedience.

Think about Jonah in the Bible who was told to go to Nineveh and give a specific message. As we read through the book of Jonah, we realize that he was never responsible for *making* the people of Nineveh turn from sin. He was only responsible for delivering what God said to whom He said it. Not doing so right away is one of the things that landed Jonah in the belly of a big fish (Jonah 1:17).

Jonah's lack of initial obedience was because he started to regard all the *what if*s as more important than God's *what did*—meaning *what did* God say?

Sometimes our greatest barrier to taking leaps is our own agenda and expectations. When we read the first three chapters of Jonah, it isn't clearly known if he had his own agenda and expectations; however, when we get to chapter 4, the truth is revealed. Jonah 4:2–3 says,

> And he prayed to the LORD and said, "O LORD, is not this what I said when I was yet in my country? That is why I made haste to flee to Tarshish; for I knew that you are a gracious God and merciful, slow to anger and abounding in steadfast love, and relenting from disaster. Therefore now, O LORD, please take my life from me, for it is better for me to die than to live."

Although Jonah did go and deliver the message to the people, he still had his own expectations of how God should handle things. These passages show us that Jonah expected God to handle the Ninevites by destroying them in order for him to be the messenger. It was as if he was saying, "God, I will do it but only if You destroy the people. However, I don't think you will, so I won't." Wow, that was such a cocky and unwise posture for a man of God to carry. Yet many of us—me included—have had to repent (or should consider doing so) for having this same attitude toward God.

As the story of Jonah continues, we learn that Jonah—still angry—left Nineveh to find a place with some shade to sit under. God, in His kindness, appointed a plant for Jonah to sit under for shade and comfort. This temporarily changed Jonah's demeanor from angry to joyful, until God later sent a worm to attack the plant and it died. Jonah again spews out angry words of frustration and death; however, God's response was powerful and compassionate:

> But God said to Jonah, "Do you do well to be angry for the plant?" And he said, "Yes, I do well to be angry, angry enough to die." And the LORD said, "You pity the plant, for which you did not labor, nor did you make it grow, which came into being in a night and perished in a night. And should not I pity Nineveh, that great city, in which there are more than 120,000 persons who do not know their right hand from their left, and also much cattle?" (Jonah 4:9–11)

And the entire book ends after God spoke those words. Interestingly enough, I believe this book was less about Jonah and the "whale," and more about Jonah and the *wail*. I believe that God wanted us to see how Jonah wailed and wanted his way so badly that he was willing to risk his life and others' lives just to get it. Jonah became the story of *what if* rather than the story of *what did*.

What will your story be?

BARRIERS OR HURDLES

One day, on my way to speak at a workshop, an attendee stopped to talk to me. He was sharing the story of his long-awaited writing journey and how it seemed like life kept slowing him down from reaching his writing goals. He said that at some point, he had to determine if what was happening was a barrier that was blocking his path or a hurdle that he was meant to jump over. The track mom in me understood very well what he was saying.

As we prepare to take leaps, there will be moments along the way when we have to pause and consider this same thing. While a barrier is something that stops or blocks us from progressing forward—a hurdle isn't intended to stop us, it just requires us to use a different method or strategy to proceed. Often, as we saw with Nehemiah earlier in the chapter, our petitions can turn a situation from a barrier that blocks into a hurdle that halts.

Some barriers will be self-imposed, while some are caused by others. Some will be sudden, while others will rise slowly. Often what feels like a barrier is actually an unexpected delay . . . and some delays are divine redirections.

In chapter 2, I shared about my desire to live in a warmer climate. After much consideration and confirmation, my husband and I decided to start the process of moving. We made phone calls, flew to the state we were considering buying a home in, had the necessary conversations with family and friends, and started to prepare our hearts, emotionally, for this adventure. Everything seemed to be moving along well until one winter morning.

I'd just dropped off the kids at school, pulled into our driveway, and opened the garage after chatting on the phone with my husband. As I walked into the house, I was reminded that my kitchen needed cleaning but decided I'd work on it after checking some emails. While I headed toward the living room, I heard a loud *boom*. My heart immediately dropped as my first thought was that something had caught fire or blown up in the house.

Quickly, I ran back through the kitchen and glanced toward

the window where I now saw smoke coming from the side of the house. I grabbed my purse, keys, and cellphone off the table and ran out into the cold, snowy day. Looking to my left, I saw the most unexpected sight—a car had crashed into the side of my house. I thought I was dreaming. Was this really happening?

So many thoughts ran through my mind. Was the car about to blow up? Was the driver okay? How did this happen?

I called the police right away as I cautiously approached the car, snow up to my calves and concern gripping my heart. The driver wasn't moving. What was I about to see? Was the person alive? Thankfully she suddenly looked up. Her face wore a look of confusion and pure disbelief, which gave my heart much-needed relief. She rolled the window down as I called to her, "Are you okay?"

"Yes," she exclaimed. "Please call for help."

After what seemed like a lifetime, the police, ambulance, fire department, and everyone else in the world arrived at the scene (including my husband). For hours, I sat in my car while people from various agencies came to investigate and make sure the house was not about to collapse.

This scene only happens on TV, *until it happens in real life.*

Thankfully, everyone, including the driver, was safe; however, life had just taken quite a turn. It's kind of hard to sell a house that someone has crashed into until it's fixed, and that process was about to take months.[3]

Was this a barrier or a hurdle?

Honestly, I don't know quite yet. What I do know is that we had to pause our move for an unknown period of time. And when I asked God why, I kept feeling drawn to the story of Abraham and Isaac (Gen. 22:1–19). Maybe God wanted to see if we would be willing to be outrageously obedient if He asked us.

I also learned that when we are presented with situations that seem outside our control and are hindering us from moving forward with our leap, it can be tempting to give up and walk away, question if we heard God right, or feel like we misunderstood His direction. But I want to give you a final piece of wisdom: pause and pray. God may have a different way He wants you to get to that end goal or even a different end goal altogether. He may be trying to produce something greater in you, like courage to fight against the enemy or strength to endure and wait. Or He might want to teach you to "trust God even when you can't trace Him," as my friend Eric would say.

CHAPTER 14

Your Propel

We are now in the final moments of our time together, and I hope I have done a good job of helping you prepare for your leap as I shared parts of my story and others'. And since you have made it to this point in the book, I have a feeling I may know a few things about you as well. If I had to guess, maybe you started reading this book to motivate and encourage you to do something you knew God called you to do. Perhaps your response to that call has been delay rather than immediate obedience.

I also suspect that you're feeling a fresh motivation and conviction regarding your leap, and you're wondering what your next step should be. After years of coming alongside people who have felt a nudge to obey God but have yet to do so, I can almost guarantee that all this excitement, conviction, and obedience won't create action in themselves. You will need something more.

See, there is a bridge that connects what we know and what we do, and my hope is that these final chapters will take you from information and motivation to action and execution. That said, I hope you can take a little tough love because what I say may feel like some tough love.

It wouldn't be right for me to spend months and months writing this book—and you to spend hours reading or listening to it—and not give you some clear practical ways to move forward. I like to call this action of moving forward "execution." Whenever I'm coaching or mentoring someone and we get to the end of our time together, one of my greatest joys is to see them actually implement what they learned through execution. I don't want them to simply take the information in like a "Sunday-only" sermon: we take thorough notes from the sermon, leave church on a heavenly high, and never pick the notebook back up to read and apply what was said. Sure, we may recall a few things from the sermon, but the message can easily become seeds thrown on rocky or thorny ground.

Why spend all that time taking notes in church, never to look back at them? If they were important enough for us to write, shouldn't they be important enough to reflect upon?

The truth is that we have trained ourselves to receive instruction from God in the same way. We hear it, write it, agree with it, and then put it on the shelf or nightstand. We are in the habit of not going back to what He said or taking action with it.

THE TRAINING GROUND OF TRANSITION

Throughout the Bible, we see God bring transition that propels people to take leaps in four ways—inconveniences, divine encounters, "suddenly moments," and instructions. Let's explore each of these and how we can water their seeds in our life.

The Power of Inconveniences

Transitions led by inconveniences often threaten our comfort but lead us to our calling. They take life as we know it and turn it upside down. We see this in Nehemiah's story as he is moved from king's cupbearer to leader of rebuilding the wall. Since Nehemiah was not just a cupbearer, but a cupbearer for the royal court, it afforded him certain comforts that others who served the king didn't have. Presenting the leave request to the king threatened these comforts in many ways. But what we learn from this story is that it won't always be convenient when God calls us to do something. However, let's recall Isaiah 55:9, regarding how God's thoughts and His ways are higher than ours. Nehemiah chose to be inconvenienced for the call, and because of that choice, he was able to do the work in little time with little delay.

Listen, I'm not going to sugarcoat this: living a surrendered life isn't easy. If it were, everyone would be doing it. Sin is easy, but surrender is sacrificial. Nehemiah understood the impact of both surrender and sacrifice.

Comfort and consecration are not companions in this life. We have to choose one or the other. That's why we are told to deny ourselves, pick up our cross, and follow Jesus (see Matt. 16:24). To deny ourselves is an act of surrender and an acknowledgment that we will be inconvenienced for the sake of the gospel and the will of our heavenly Father. Our willingness to be inconvenienced lets God know that He has first and final say in our lives, which is exactly what He needs in order to propel us for His glory. God can use those inconveniences to move us along the path that leads to His perfect will in our lives, just as He did with Nehemiah.

Now, let's talk about the second way God will propel us—through encounters.

An Encounter with Jesus

Is there someone in your life who, if they told you they surrendered their life to Christ, it might be challenging to trust or believe them? Who has a tendency to manipulate emotions, is selfish rather than selfless, and never sees anything wrong with their destructive behavior or patterns? We all know that person with whom we have had to set boundaries to protect our peace and at times our safety.

Well, Saul was that person for the Jews. A moment in his presence could mean destruction for innocent followers of Jesus. Yet one day, he encountered Jesus on the road to Damascus (see Acts 9), and it was this encounter that changed the course of his life, his eternity, and our story. Saul, also known as Paul, became a surrendered servant of the Lord. His life was marked by a moment of encounter that led him to the truth of Jesus Christ and a realization that his actions toward the Jews who believed in Jesus as the Messiah displeased God. This is the nature of true encounters with God. It transforms our life and brings us into a place of awe, wonder, and obedience.

If we are in Christ, we all have a "road to Damascus" moment that should lead us to obedience. Reading this book may be that moment for you, but you may be able to point to another. These are defining moments in life where God is making His instructions very clear to us. We can ignore them, but we can't escape them, and they often lead us right into a major leap that we didn't anticipate.

It reminds me of a time when I was chatting with my rideshare driver. Often, I can determine how much I might enjoy a city by how kind, friendly, and welcoming the drivers are. One day, while heading to an airport with two of my children, I noticed that the driver was playing a faith-based station. In my experience, this isn't common; I was immediately intrigued by it and started talking to the driver about music. He seemed excited to meet a fellow Christian and started to share his conversion story with me.

"I really think Christian music is a gateway to Christianity," he said. I wasn't sure what he meant until he went on to explain: "I was a practicing Hindu and honestly poked fun at Christians. One day, I came across some Christian music and thought it was really good, so I started playing it, although I still thought Christianity was crazy. During this time, I often struggled with some very bad thoughts." I could tell he wasn't being specific because my kids were around. He continued, "These thoughts would often consume me, and although I'd said all the Hindu prayers, nothing helped. I was confused because I knew how to pray the prayers. I was so committed to Hinduism that I was about to become a Hindu priest."

As he continued to talk, he shared how one day he was in one of the darkest places of his life and the weight of the struggle was burying him. He'd said all the prayers and chants, and nothing worked. So, he decided to say a quick prayer that he honestly didn't think would work either. He said, "Jesus, if You are real, please come and help me." It was at that moment that he felt something go through his entire body, and from that day forward, he never had a dark thought again like he had in the past.

Now he serves the Lord and shares the love of Jesus with others as often as he can.

This is the power of an encounter that will propel us into the will of God.

Just Like That

Another way we are propelled is by what I call "suddenly moments." I've talked to numerous people who have told me that their leap happened suddenly and unexpectedly. This seems to completely go against our plan-the-future thinking, but it happens to be a very common way that God will bring about transition.

We have become averse to sudden change, and understandably so. In a culture where we are taught the value of routine, structure, and planning, the word *suddenly* can create a sense of anxiety and uncertainty. But when these unplanned moments present them-selves to us by way of God's perfect plan, we should reconsider our perspective.

Peter going from a fisherman to a disciple was a suddenly mo-ment. One minute he was trying to catch fish, and *suddenly* Jesus loads up his net with more fish than he can drag back to shore. That moment was an invitation for Peter to make a leap. It was an invitation to go with Jesus on a three-year mission that would change the trajectory of Peter's life and story. Our suddenly is an invitation as well. Suddenly moments have the power to shift us from what *was* into what *will be* if we respond in obedience.

A few years back my husband had prayed about getting a specific type of job within the print industry as he began to prepare to return to full-time work. He spent many nights and days applying for jobs that fit the description, and ones that didn't, and nothing seemed to come through. However, one day while running an errand, he received a random call. Someone had found his résumé online and was looking for the exact skills he had in the exact type of job he wanted. We both thought it was a prank or a fake call. We put them on hold and researched the company. Turns out they were com-pletely legitimate, and the job offer was as well.

That suddenly moment was a huge blessing to our family and ended my husband's Builder's Leap season as he returned to the workforce after four years of pause to launch the ministry as well as our design and printing business.

So how can we prepare our heart and mind for a leap by way of suddenly? Start by meditating on the Word. Then we can ac-knowledge God's suddenly moments are full of sweet surprises and special gifts because He loves us, and His nature is good.

Where You Go, I Go

This is probably one of the easiest concepts to understand, but the hardest to obey. Sometimes our leap will come by way of clear instructions that we don't want to follow. These instructions may not be easy or fun even when they come from God.

It makes me think of an interview I had with a podcast guest, Kaela McKaig. During our time together, she made a very powerful statement as she talked about her transition from the United States back to Canada to care for her father and start her podcast, *His Word My Walk*. She said, "God has opened these doors [because] I didn't really say yes; I said okay. And He worked with my okay because He knew how hard it was for me to get to that point."[1]

When she shared this, it truly gave me a shift in perspective regarding leaps. I realized that God can still work with our hesitant obedience. Sometimes we feel like we have to be head-over-heels in love with the leap God is calling us to make. But we even see with Jesus before He went to the cross that He wasn't. He said, "My Father, if it be possible, let this cup pass from me; nevertheless, not as I will, but as you will" (Matt. 26:39).

Jesus understood the instructions and was willing to be obedient, yet He dealt with the inner turmoil of its difficulty and His desire to do it.

When God gives us instructions about our leap, we should take them, pray over them, and ask God for the strength to follow through with them.

PROPEL FOR PURPOSE

Lately, flying hasn't felt the same. I used to love the drive to the airport, going through the security line, and the noise of people rushing about as they hurried to their terminal. It seemed like everyone was on a mission, and many were excited about the journey. But over the past few years, I've started to not enjoy the experience as much.

What once was an exciting and peaceful time has become an anxiety-inducing and exhausting one. The multiple layovers, high food prices, and frequent flight cancellations have made me want to load up my minivan and drive from here to Timbuktu. Delays aren't fun because they can make the trip take longer, cost more money, and slow us down from getting to the destination.

But you know what keeps me waiting at airports, getting on planes, and praying through turbulence? God's purpose.

God is propelling us for His divine purpose through our leaps.

I know that each time I fly, I am on mission—be it family time or ministry—to help people encounter the truth of Jesus. Each time the plane is propelled into the air, it is taking me on a new assignment where I will learn something, meet someone, and grow somehow.

Here is the thing: God is propelling us for His divine purpose through our leaps. Although we may experience life turbulence along the way, we have the honor of traveling near and far on behalf of the Creator of the world. This journey was established from the beginning of time with the beautiful ending of our leap into heaven's gates.

I don't want you to walk away thinking that being propelled into the leap is going to always be easy, desirable, or fun. But I also don't want you to anticipate that it won't be. There are so many beautiful, historic, and glorious moments that come from any act of obedience. Nehemiah rebuilding the wall, Abraham being promised descendants that outnumbered the stars, Peter becoming the rock of the church, and Paul paving the way for us as Gentiles to be adopted into the body of Christ. All their leaps propelled them so far that we're still speaking about them today.

Now let me ask you . . .

What life-changing moments are you anticipating as you leap for the glory of God?

The Principle of Perseverance

My oldest daughter's years in middle school were difficult, to say the least. As a mom, watching her go through social and academic challenges and adjustments often brought tears to my eyes. I was concerned that so many hits in such a short period of time would break her spirit. Oftentimes, I tried to encourage her, but I wasn't quite sure if what I said was actually helpful. Nonetheless, despite how she felt about what was going on around her or within her, I tried to always point her to truth and speak life.

However, during that season, I noticed something about my daughter that brought a great peace to my mama heart: she didn't give up easily. It was as if she had this innate ability to press through the difficulty, hurt, and disappointment to persevere. When her friend group completely stopped talking to her due to a misunderstanding, leaving her completely friendless for a season, she steadied herself. When she studied all night for a test but received disappointing results, she didn't give up.

God's power worked through her to help her overcome every challenge, letdown, hard assignment, and loss. This strength went beyond simply being self-motivated—it was another level of endurance that can't be explained.

When her middle school graduation rolled around, we celebrated her! As we waited for the students to come out, a slideshow was displayed in the auditorium of each graduate. Each student had a photo and a quote, and as I sat in anticipation of my daughter (who *has* to have a last name that would be toward the end of the alphabet), her photo finally popped up. When I saw her smile, it was bright and hopeful and next to her beautiful picture it read, "Future Occupation: Child Advocate. Favorite Quote: 'When writing the story of life, don't let anyone else hold the pen.' Harley-Davidson."[1]

Suddenly, I understood why God had gifted her with such tenacity, determination, strength, resilience, and perseverance. She is called to the saving and advocacy of children. She must understand their story, their struggles, and their buried strengths.

I'm so proud of my daughter because she allowed the things that tried to break her to build her instead. She also taught me through her journey that perseverance is a doorway that allows us to fulfill our purpose and walk in our assignment.

DEFINING THE PRINCIPLE

As followers of Jesus, we are marked by our ability to endure and persevere until the end (see Matt. 24:13). Our choice to be made whole by the truth of God's Word and to live out the evidence of its transformative power gives us what we need to fulfill this assignment.

When I think of the many leapers who have gone before me; from biblical times to modern day, I find a common thread of obedience, sacrifice, and perseverance.

Over the years, I have done many leaps—more than I could mention in this book. No matter the leaps I've made, I've had to understand this principle of perseverance.

My definition is different from what an online search engine or dictionary may say. My definition is provided through the powerful words of the apostle Paul who says in Philippians 3:14, "I press on toward the goal for the prize of the upward call of God in Christ Jesus."

This is what the principle of perseverance means: to press toward the goal that God has set before us, no matter the cost, because of the call. It's a place of surrender, sacrifice, and strength.

Perseverance means: to press toward the goal that God has set before us, no matter the cost, because of the call. It's a place of surrender, sacrifice, and strength.

As we end our time together, I want to share two final things that I believe will help you as you take the 5 leaps: songs and Scripture. Both of these are intended to give you an anchor as you plan, prepare, and execute your next leap of faith. Ask God to lead you to songs that will bring life and encouragement to you. When you identify the songs God wants stamped upon your heart and you meditate on the Scriptures He has for the journey ahead, you will see the evidence of His presence upon the path He has set before you.

We are not doing this for the sake of taking risk; we're doing this for God's glory to be revealed upon the earth. I think Albaner C. Eugene Jr. said it best, "God wants our stories to end with, 'to God be the glory!'"[2]

So how do we press toward that goal no matter the cost? We must have a firm foundation to help us endure.

A Song to Help You Stand

Have you ever woken up and had a worship song on replay in your mind?

Or listened to a song and the memory connected to the melody brought hope and encouragement to you during a season of trial or transition?

When this happens, I believe these are precious moments when God is singing a love song over us so that we can know He is present in whatever we're enduring. This has happened to me on numerous occasions, and each time, the song points me toward the truth and nature of Jesus.

Music has a way of speaking to the heart of a matter, and the right kind of music will speak life, hope, and courage. That is why I find it so important to have a song to stand on when we are taking leaps. It can be an older or newer song, a contemporary hit or a hymn. Whatever you choose, it should remind you of the consistent nature of God in this ever-changing and often uncertain world. That is how I feel about the hymn, "My Hope Is Built on Nothing Less." This song reminds me that my hope in Christ will carry me no matter the cost or circumstance. This truth and God's love for us is what our hope should be built upon.

My hope is built on nothing less
Than Jesus' blood and righteousness;
I dare not trust the sweetest frame,
But wholly lean on Jesus' name.

On Christ, the solid Rock, I stand;
All other ground is sinking sand,
All other ground is sinking sand.

When darkness veils His lovely face,
I rest on His unchanging grace;
In every high and stormy gale,
My anchor holds within the veil.[3]

Scriptures to Stand On

Below are verses from Scripture that will be gentle and humble reminders of God's love and faithfulness along the journey. Treasure these in your heart and meditate on them day and night. Let them become your first point of reference and your weapon in the battle to the finish. These verses and a description of how to use them are also provided as a download at rachelgscott.com/scripturestostandon.

- 2 Thessalonians 3:3: "But the Lord is faithful. He will establish you and guard you against the evil one."
- Ecclesiastes 11:6: "In the morning sow your seed, and at evening withhold not your hand, for you do not know which will prosper, this or that, or whether both alike will be good."
- Joshua 1:9: "Have I not commanded you? Be strong and courageous. Do not be frightened, and do not be dismayed, for the LORD your God is with you wherever you go."
- Philippians 1:6: "And I am sure of this, that he who began a good work in you will bring it to completion at the day of Jesus Christ."
- Matthew 19:26: "But Jesus looked at them and said, 'With man this is impossible, but with God all things are possible.'"
- Deuteronomy 31:8: "It is the LORD who goes before you. He will be with you; he will not leave you or forsake you. Do not fear or be dismayed."

- Romans 8:31: "What then shall we say to these things? If God is for us, who can be against us?"
- Proverbs 3:5–6: "Trust in the LORD with all your heart, and do not lean on your own understanding. In all your ways acknowledge him, and he will make straight your paths."
- Psalm 32:8: "I will instruct you and teach you in the way you should go; I will counsel you with my eye upon you."
- 1 John 5:14: "And this is the confidence that we have toward him, that if we ask anything according to his will he hears us."

As you boldly take leaps of faith, know that God is with you, He is for you, and He will not let you down. My prayer for you is the same as Paul's when he spoke to the church of Thessalonica:

So we keep on praying for you, asking our God to enable you to live a life worthy of his call. May he give you the power to accomplish all the good things your faith prompts you to do. Then the name of our Lord Jesus will be honored because of the way you live, and you will be honored along with him. This is all made possible because of the grace of our God and Lord, Jesus Christ. (2 Thess. 1:11–12 NLT)

Taking the Leaps Quiz

To help you identify the natural inclination you have as a leaper, take this quiz I created at rachelgscott.com/takingthe5leapsquiz. This tool, and everything you've learned in this book about taking a leap based on your situational need, will help equip you to make a change and answer God's call.

It's time to take your next leap!

Acknowledgments

E very good and perfect gift is from above (James 1:17). God, it's an honor to be used for your glory to write words of truth, courage, and hope. Thank you for choosing me to be a voice in this hour for the people who need to be reminded of the hope and faith found in you.

To my husband, Willie, thank you for making space for me to write. From cooking dinner for the family when I needed to wrap up a chapter (your staple chicken, rice, and broccoli) to sending me off to a hotel so I could meet deadlines. Your words of encouragement, support, and prayers have always been such a wonderful gift to me. I love you so much.

To my Dad, thank you for always being a present father and grandfather. For coming over and watching the kids so that Willie and I could get caught up on writing and work. For having a library of books for me to borrow as I wrote my own and being a safe space for me to share my heart and celebrate exciting moments as if they were your own. But most importantly, thank you for covering me in prayer and teaching me how to draw near to God. You're truly the best dad a girl could ask for.

To my Mom, thank you for blazing the trail of ministry for me and for the sweet reminders that you are proud of me. Thank you for always speaking life into me and for pointing me to Jesus since birth.

Dominique, Darius, Gabby, and Aaron, I'm so honored to be called your mother. I'm so proud of all of you and the gifts God has placed in you. I pray that my ceiling is your floor and you go to places with God far beyond where I could have ever gone. Thank you for your patience with me through the writing process. I love each of you as only a mother could.

Autumn, Willie, and Antonio, thank you for allowing me to share in your world as a mother figure and celebrating with me. You motivate me in more ways than you will ever know, and I love you all.

To my sisters, Neisey and Leah, I don't know what I would do without you two. You're my sisters by birth but best friends by choice. You both have encouraged, supported, comforted, laughed with, and come alongside me in this writing journey like I could have never imagined. Your life is evidence of God's love for me and I thank Him for you two. He knew I needed amazing sisters, and He gave me you.

To Eric "Bro" Graves, Maria, Janelle, Courtnaye, Lauren, Ebony, and Sharon, each of you have been true friends to me in the most amazing ways before and during this process. Your prayers, support, honesty, motivation, time, feedback, and encouragement have been a blessing to me in this season and so many others. You all know the spiritual attack that came right when this journey began and you held my arms up through it all. I pray that God multiplies His blessing in your lives because of the blessing you have been in mine.

To Darrell, thank you for counseling and pastoring me during this exciting and difficult season. You always knew which hat I needed you to wear whenever we talked, and you always did it with grace and love. Thank you for showing me what it looks like to be a leader with the heart of Jesus.

Thank you to my dynamic manuscript development team, launch community, and author community whose feedback was invaluable and whose support was appreciated.

Thank you to my agent, editors, marketing team, and all of the Moody staff. You took a chance on me and this book and I'm so grateful for you. I pray that God gets the glory out of it.

And last but not least, thank you to every leaper who reads and shares this book. I pray that it transforms you and those around you for decades to come. I pray the words and the message bring life to your soul, draw you closer to God, and ignite a fire in you to live a leaping lifestyle.

Notes

CHAPTER 1: FROM CALLING TO VISION

1. Andy Stanley, *Visioneering: Your Guide for Discovering and Maintaining Personal Vision* (Colorado Springs: Multnomah, 2016), 19.

CHAPTER 2: THE VEHICLE OF A VISION

1. Hannah Hurnard, *Hinds' Feet on High Places* (Wheaton, IL: Living Books, 1986), 8.

CHAPTER 3: THE PURPOSE OF IT ALL

1. *Cambridge Dictionary*, s.v. "purpose (*n.*)," https://dictionary.cambridge.org/us/dictionary/english/purpose.
2. *Merriam-Webster Thesaurus*, s.v. "assignment (*n.*)," https://www.merriam-webster.com/thesaurus/assignment.

CHAPTER 4: THE SETUP

1. Rachel G. Scott, "Interview with Steven Adjei," *The Five Leaps* podcast, season 4, episode 49, www.the5leaps.com.
2. "Bible Timeline: Chronological Index of the Years and Times from Adam Unto Christ," Houston Christian University, April 11, 2016,

https://hc.edu/museums/dunham-bible-museum/tour-of-the-museum/
bible-in-america/bibles-for-a-young-republic/chronological-index-of-
the-years-and-times-from-adam-unto-christ/#:~:text=So%2069%20
weeks%20amount%20to,of%20Christ%2C%20unto%20this%20present.

3. Michael Vanlaningham, "Matthew," in Michael Rydelnik and Michael Vanlaningham, eds., *The Moody Bible Commentary* (Chicago: Moody, 2014), 1471.

CHAPTER 5: FAVOR ABOVE FEAR

1. *Merriam-Webster*, s.v. "speculate (*v.*)," https://www.merriam-webster.com/dictionary/speculate.
2. *Merriam-Webster*, s.v. "imagination (*n.*)," https://www.merriam-webster.com/dictionary/imaginations.
3. *Merriam-Webster*, s.v. "thoughts (*n.*)," https://www.merriam-webster.com/dictionary/thoughts.
4. Amy McKenna, "15 Nelson Mandela Quotes," *Encyclopedia Britannica*, January 31, 2018, https://www.britannica.com/list/nelson-mandela-quotes.

CHAPTER 6: THE FISHERMAN'S LEAP

1. Rachel G. Scott, "Interview with Kevin Anselmo," February 22, 2023, *The Five Leaps* podcast, 37:03, https://taking-the-leap-with-rachel-g-scott.simplecast.com/episodes/kevin-anselmo.

CHAPTER 7: THE SHEPHERD'S LEAP

1. Elisabeth Elliot, *Joyful Surrender: 7 Disciplines for the Believer's Life* (Grand Rapids, MI: Revell, 1982), 35.
2. Ibid.
3. "Genesis," in Michael Rydelnik and Michael Vanlangingham, eds., *The Moody Bible Commentary* (Chicago: Moody, 2014), 68.
4. Rachel G. Scott, "Interview with Brandi Morris," October 5, 2022, *The Five Leaps* podcast, 29:39, https://taking-the-leap-with-rachel-g-scott.simplecast.com/episodes/brandi-morris.

CHAPTER 8: THE BUILDER'S LEAP

1. "Why Was It Important to Rebuild the Walls Around Jerusalem?," GotQuestions.org, December 4, 2014, https://www.gotquestions.org/rebuild-walls-Jerusalem.html.
2. Rich Wilkerson Jr., "It's Okay to Not Be Okay," YouTube Video, 0:50, August 10, 2020, https://www.youtube.com/watch?v=QhOryIPwnU8.
3. The Gospel Coalition, "How to Teach Children and Youth the Gospel Story," YouTube, 48:52, March 24, 2014, https://www.youtube.com/watch?v=zFKqMUrUCNo.

CHAPTER 9: THE TENTMAKER'S LEAP

1. Aaron Kuecker, "Tent Making and Christian Life," *Theology of Work Bible Commentary*, 2012, https://www.theologyofwork.org/new-testament/acts/a-clash-of-kingdoms-community-and-powerbrokers-acts-13-19/tent-making-and-christian-life-acts-181-4.

CHAPTER 10: THE TRAILBLAZER'S LEAP

1. *Merriam-Webster*, s.v. "trailblazer (*n.*)," https://www.merriam-webster.com/dictionary/trailblazer.
2. Rachel G. Scott, "Years of Silent Nights (Pt. 1)," I Can't Come Down (blog), December 4, 2022, https://icantcomedown.com/2022/12/04/400-years-of-silent-nights-pt-1/.

CHAPTER 11: YOUR PRAYER PLAN

1. A portion of the opening of this chapter also appears in the author's online devotional, "Uncomplicating Prayer," YouVersion, https://www.bible.com/reading-plans/27693-uncomplicating-barrier-simplifying-conversation/day/1.

CHAPTER 13: YOUR PETITION

1. *Merriam-Webster*, s.v. "petition," https://www.merriam-webster.com/dictionary/petition.

2. Commentary on Nehemiah 2:2, Biblehub.com, https://biblehub.com/commentaries/nehemiah/2-2.htm.

3. A portion of the opening of this section also appears in the author's online blog, "The Tutoring of Unexpected Transition (Pt. 1)," I Can't Come Down, https://icantcomedown.com/2022/02/14/the-tutoring-of-unexpected-transition-pt-1/.

CHAPTER 14: YOUR PROPEL

1. Rachel G. Scott, "Interview with Kaela McKaig," May 23, 2023, *The Five Leaps* podcast, 29:41, https://taking-the-leap-with-rachel-g-scott.simplecast.com/episodes/kaela-mckaig.

APPENDIX: THE PRINCIPLE OF PERSEVERANCE

1. Quote from Harley Davidson, "When Writing the Story of Your Life, Don't Let Anyone Else Hold the Pen," Quotespedia.org, May 10, 2020, https://www.quotespedia.org/authors/h/harley-davidson/when-writing-the-story-of-your-life-dont-let-anyone-else-hold-the-pen-harley-davidson/.

2. Albaner C. Eugene Jr., "Just Finish," Instagram (@thisisalbaner), May 2023, https://www.instagram.com/reel/CsWJFa3Air9/.

3. Edward Mote, "My Hope Is Built on Nothing Less," *The Baptist Hymnal 1991*, 406; Hymnary.org, hymnary.org/text/my_hope_is_built_on_nothing_less.

What if you don't have *a calling* from God . . .
but *callings?*

Isn't it time you said *yes* to God?

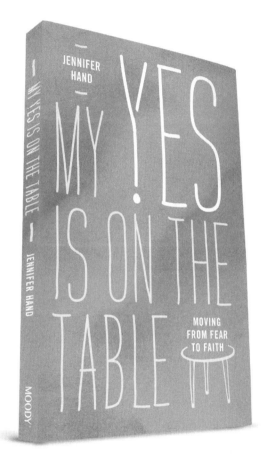